# "The
## Book
Of
# Reframes…"

# "The
# Book
## Of
# Reframes…"

*By Stewart Robertson, BSc*

## Thank you

I'd like to thank you for purchasing The Book Of Reframes! You will find it an ideal resource, in or out of the therapy room.

I also want to invite you to join me on my newsletter where I discuss free stress tips, EFT pilot studies, META-Medicine®, tapping tips, and much more. You can view it here:

### http://www.StressReliefClinic.co.uk/Newsletter.html

I love you all and there's absolutely nothing you can do about it!

– Stewart Robertson

First published in 2008 by Lulu.

ISBN 978 1 4092 0417 6

For further information about Stewart Robertson products and services, visit http://www.StressReliefClinic.co.uk

For Lynne, (1972-2007), my sibling spirit on a human endeavour.

# Table Of Contents

# Part 3 – Live Examples

# Foreword

I think from an emotional point of view, many of us wander through life, accumulating troublesome memories, resentments, fear, painful associations, etc, not really knowing what to do about it. Unfortunately, when these issues go unchecked long enough, disease becomes a very real possibility. My specialty is in serious disease, and, for me, it's only these unresolved emotional issues that can explain the rocketing levels of diabetes, cancer, heart disease, autism, allergies, ADHD, etc, showing up in our society today.

With the proper application of EFT however, we can remove all of that. Both reframing and EFT have their own benefits when used individually. But used together, the end result far exceeds the sum of the parts.

This is a simple book. A simple idea, and one whose time has come. Stewart has amassed a lot of experience in a clinic setting, and so speaks to you from the front lines. I think it was on the first international EFT Masterclass in London that Stewart approached me for guidance on reframing with EFT. So, in this book, it's clear that the student has now become the teacher!

Distilling the essence of reframing, with its roots in intuition, can be tricky. Captured in these pages is the reframing *process* as well as many actual reframes to use in practice. I'm not suggesting you apply all the info herein verbatim, but there's certainly enough here to get you to a place of reframing expertise that much faster, should you wish to. I trained Stewart through Levels 1, 2 & 3 of EFT, and I've seen him progress dramatically in that time. The depth of his knowledge, that he retells for us here, is obvious.

During my courses, I sometimes see trainees struggle to find *just the right* reframe; or those who are so clearly trying to think ahead, that they lose all rapport with the client. A quality reframe can help loosen a problem dramatically; but the trick is allowing your intuition to show you which reframe will hit the mark, in the flow of a session. Gift your client a reframe that is intuitive, from the heart, and 100% for their benefit. They can tell the difference.

I think my favourite reframe is on Gary Craig's DVD Borrowing Benefits series. He's working with Stacey Vornbrock, a sports coach, on blocks of rejection. Stacey has difficulty current day in approaching sports professionals for work opportunities, and they're working with a specific memory. It involves a boy at high school, who rejected her romantically. Gary leads her in to a setup ...*Even though, I am a prisoner, to a 16 year-old boy's words, and at this age, I wouldn't take a 16 year-old boy's words or advice on anything!!*....classic Gary.

This book has a wealth of resources. You will find it a great companion along your path toward mastery of EFT or your preferred therapy. Use it wisely, at your pace, and whatever comes up for you along the way…TAP ON IT!

Love & hugs,

- **Karl Dawson, EFT Master**
  **http://www.efttrainingcourses.net**

# Part 1: Introduction

# ~ 1 ~

# Important Introduction

## *Starting Out*

When I started out in this field I was not what you might call a natural reframer. But through watching many of the Masters work I recognised the enormous leverage reframing gives us over our own issues. I needed a reference point where I could learn multiple ideas until I became a natural myself.

I needed a transparent source of reframes, from an everyday therapist on the ground, who was not being filmed or publicised or demoing or branded or productised in some way. A resource that the average therapist could use and that everyone could understand. At the time that wasn't available, so I decided to compile my own stash of new perspectives to use with clients. And you're reading the results.

Within these pages it is my intention to give you as much practical and useable material as I can. It has been compiled from the extensive study of many (many) master therapists at work.

## Overview

In part 1, I will give you an overview of reframing, and why it's useful in the first place. You'll be interested to read my observations on the use of reframing alongside EFT (Emotional Freedom Techniques), and in addition why the basic EFT routines work so well.

Of course, much of the skill of reframing is in the delivery, and in Chapter 4 I will tell you how I personally use specific language to do so effectively, and I offer you a specific framework into which you can insert your own reframe, for perfect results every time. I also explain in detail my Top 5 hand-picked reframes I use with highest hit-rates in the clinic, for dissolving the most stubborn objections.

Part 2 contains a specific framework for you to work backwards from your client's presenting emotion, to a specific, highly-targeted reframe. I've called this method the Emotional Levels of Therapy™. And in Chapters 8 and 9 I present the reframes themselves. I've categorised them by type of emotion, the easiest way I have found.

I've written this material from the perspective of someone using EFT, my favourite healing modality. But the reframes and concepts can be used with the same effectiveness with *any* therapy of your choice. Naturally, I can only ever explain things from my own experience, and this book is intended as a personal perspective at all times, just one version of events, and not THE version of events.

I presuppose in these pages that you are a budding therapist of at least a little experience, and so I speak of rapport, association/dissociation, modalities, and submodalities etc without further explanation.

Reading ahead you will find certain angles and reframes which don't necessarily fall under the "correct" heading, such is the nature of this material. However, I include them all, as each have met with some success in my own experience, and therefore may be useful to you. Some items may be used for several different types of emotion your client is experiencing. In this case I have listed the item under the category I most commonly use it. Naturally your experience may be different. The categories I've used are my suggestions only. Of course you should feel free to mix and match the reframes herein according to the therapy plan and situation; I always try to customise to my client as far as possible.

Bear in mind that as you choose from the many reframes herein, it often takes just one nicely timed and delivered reframe, with rapport, to turn a session around and help your client begin the healing process in earnest.

Bear in mind also, that some of these reframes won't seem to fully make sense on paper, as they are intended for use in the free-flowing setting of a therapeutic session. Once you have inserted the client's problem content (*always* in their words) you will appreciate the contrast within the reframe and hence the statement will make sense.

Start out by learning and trying just one or two at a time, perfecting your delivery and "landing success", then moving on to try others. My favourites (Chapter 6) are a good place to start your journey.

But let's not allow all this reframing to cloud our vision. For if all we did was reframe then we would be purely talk therapists. We mustn't let it distract us from the real business of EFT – which is working to allow the energy system to release blocks in the way – the reframing simply softens the vibration and paves the way for EFT to have maximum effect.

And, we can't *not* notice that our reframing does seem to land better – much better – if done whilst tapping. A new perspective offered whilst the energy circuits are flowing in the right direction enables us to absorb and reprocess new perspectives on an old situation, with grace and speed.

## *Working On You*

As with most of this work, it is always hardest for us to see our own "stuff." Being "in it" i.e. focussing on the problem, whilst trying to simultaneously be "out of it," i.e. navigating the course of the therapy session, is possibly the hardest task ever. If you are struggling to shift your issues even with all the resources in these pages, my first suggestion is always to work with someone else, and indeed this was where I started on my own journey. Outsiders looking into our world can leap logical levels laughingly and offer fresh scope and insight on our situations, leaving us free to fully reprocess the situation with new meaning, and hopefully more useful beliefs.

## *Suggestion*

As I've said, I offer most of the reframes in the book in the style of the basic EFT(Emotional Freedom Techniques) setup statement however they are also readily used with your preferred therapy technique. For the uninitiated I reproduce the basic recipe and an explanation of SUDS levels in the Appendix, which can be learned and applied within 10 minutes. For those unfamiliar with this phenomenal healing tool, I urge you to read and apply that chapter now, as one reading now will benefit you throughout the text.

# ~ 2 ~

## What Is Reframing, And Why Use It?

If I place an old boot in an art gallery, does that make it art? Is art simply anything that's in an art gallery?

Reframing, or changing the meaning of something, is the main endeavour of most psychotherapy in whatever shape or form.

Meaning itself is something that we label upon events, situations, memories etc, in an attempt to make sense of events, and more importantly, to learn from them. However, at some point, it is a safe assumption that all of us will draw some less-than-useful meanings and conclusions from the events of our lives. And by holding these decisions, meanings, and conclusions as our personal truths about these specific events, if enough events happen, or we replay it enough times, it then becomes our belief about life and the world in general, "out there."

By realising that we may have misinterpreted, we can reprocess and re-meaning the situations of our lives and arrive at more functional, useful, and congruent operating beliefs for now and the future. We can re-map our own internal territory such that future meanings automatically function in a more useful way.

## *The Purpose & Benefits Of Reframing*

Reframing generally:

- can increase rapport
- ushers into reality the cognitive shifts so typical of EFT
- can help clear the client's blocks of unwillingness, lack of self-acceptance, or desire to hold on to the problem for whatever reason
- can help the client to move the event from outside their model of the world or belief system, to inside it.

Reframing, in the context of specific trauma, can:

- help us open up (and therefore allow us to fully clear) all the *aspects* of a particular trauma and therefore do a more thorough job.
- help open up therapy into new avenues or aspects or directions to go in next.

- help the client to resolve, to rationalise, to "make rational", and to make the trauma explainable within the boundaries of their existing beliefs and model of the world.

In the case of severe trauma this last point may involve the idea of moving the location of the processed energy of the memory from the hindbrain where it is a survival-level threat, to the frontal and mid-brain; the cortical-social brain, where it can be safely processed then retained in the hippocampal long-term memory as a learning. I admit this is speculation on my part as to the fate of the energy of a processed trauma in the physical brain. But if this is the case, then we are also assisting this physical shift to take place with our reframing.

Because as long as unresolved memories are held energetically in our system, on a physical level this will manifest as an active conflict with all the related symptoms including obsessive thinking, mania, stress, hypertension, depression, cold extremities, poor sleeping patterns, and so on.

Reframing is important as it helps us directly address and recode the meanings we automatically attribute to our experiences. And as we do, we re-create better (or more useful) behaviours, responses, and emotions to those experiences in future. Our internal map of the world changes, and parts of us that were previously out of synch with the whole, realign.

## *Why Reframing With EFT?*

Luckily, one of the hallmarks of EFT is witnessing such cognitive shifts WITHOUT ever addressing such meanings directly.

Having said that, in the evolution of EFT, you will notice a change in Gary Craig's approach post-1995. From the Borrowing Benefits series onwards, you will see Gary make long rambling mini-speeches within the setup statement of the basic recipe, combining the stimulation of the energy system with reframing the meaning of events.

So that, when we apply reframing simultaneously with EFT, we are fostering into reality such cognitive shifts linguistically as well as energetically.

With EFT, a two-way street seems to exist such that:

(i) using EFT whilst reframing appears to give the reframes offered a higher hit-rate than not;

(ii) the reframes themselves seem to soften the individual's resistance and vibration regardless, and therefore enhances the effectiveness of the EFT being delivered.

## *Adaptations For Survival*

From an evolutionary perspective, we are built to adjust to circumstances and automate tasks as quickly as possible to an unconscious level, leaving as many conscious resources as possible free to deal with survival issues, predator threats etc. Usually this equates to the streamlined formation of beliefs.

This attempted automation process still takes place just the same after traumatic events. So in an attempt to survive, from an evolutionary point of view, our brains will automatically rationalise as much as possible of the trauma, and build accommodating beliefs and behavioural adjustments around what's left.

So, parts of develop which are the *adaptations* to these traumas. Whether they are adaptations or not, they still become automated very quickly, they become 'part of us'; and since they are purely the by-product of the unconscious mind's attempt to survive, they will naturally contain aspects, behaviours, recurrent emotions, ways of thinking and so on that are not necessarily beneficial or functional in our daily lives in this highly evolved, socialised society of ours. Remember that although we live in a world that is highly modernised, cultured, politicised, and technologically advanced, on a basic animal level we are still running the same survival programs that we did thousands of years ago.

At the time the trauma was processed by the client's unconscious mind, compromises in day-to-day behaviour may have been built in, obsessive behaviours, new or changed beliefs, habits, addictions, and so on - anything and everything (no matter how dysfunctional or un-useful) which will allow the creature to function and continue to survive beyond the immediate trauma at hand. That is the priority of the unconscious mind.

(sidebar – most adaptations the body and mind make are only for the highest intention of your survival, either of the immediate trauma at hand, or to ensure you survive the same trauma again in the future.)

EFT is an amazing tool. But to assume that EFT (or any therapy) will suddenly, with one application, immediately get round these built-in adaptations we have running, (which are 100% *required* and *necessary* for our survival) is naivety.

Understanding this survival mechanism built into our psychology will help you understand your client's psychological reversals, objections, and resistance, if you struggle to make progress with EFT. META-Medicine® has much more to say about the survival meaning of our behavioural adaptations. You can learn more on my site (www.StressReliefClinic.co.uk).

Therefore, reframing, or some form of rationalising, or softening, of these adjusted parts of ourselves, is almost always required, in order to make progress on the core issue.

You can understand now, that although the default setup statement is wide ranging and works for many cases, it is inevitable that much more specific reframes will be needed to help soften those parts adaptations your client has made, and thus the need for a creative toolbox (and first-class calibration skills) in this regard.

# ~ 3 ~

# When To Reframe (And When Not)

O f course every client arrives with their own beliefs and writings on their walls about what therapy will entail and where to begin. Typically, my clients are more than happy to talk (at length) about their issues and are therefore already in the problem state they are seeking to resolve. For me therefore, there is never a bad time to tap with EFT, and likewise it's difficult to say there is a bad time for a reframe. Most of the time your insights will be welcomed by the client, although not always fully internalised in their unconscious mind on the first pass.

Having said that, I offer you a variety of guidelines below, on when (and when not) reframing might be useful during a session. This includes some ground-work information you need to get started, as well as some pointers mid-delivery. More on the preconditions for reframing in Chapter 4.

## *When To Reframe*

- when you have successfully established the operating belief or perspective on the situation/memory in question and a new perspective is desired. Establish underlying belief by asking questions like:

    "What did you decide about the world and yourself as a result of this experience?"

    "What did you learn from this experience?"

    "How did this influence the rest of your life?"

- when SUDS levels (emotional intensity) stop going down but levels are ideally below 7.

- when you intuitively sense (or have muscle tested accordingly) your client is holding on to some level of emotional intensity, for some specific reason.

- when your client *knows* they are holding on to intensity for a reason but they don't consciously know why, or can't articulate why.

- when you intuitively sense your client is on the edge of a new understanding and a fresh perspective could help him/her get there quicker now.

- when you have not necessarily witnessed any obvious resistance yet, but simply want to make the path for EFT as clear as possible *anyway*, so you go straight in with a reframe.

- following some other therapeutic intervention on a specific emotional aspect or memory, which had limited success in helping the client reach new perspectives.

- when rapport is lacking, or the mood/energy of the session feels low.

- to speed up the collapse of issues or memories, even when straight EFT (or your therapy) is working fine.

## *When Not To Reframe*

- when you have already had a few or more unsuccessful attempts at reframes your client has not "bought." Additional attempts at this stage will likely be met with further resistance as your client closes off, not only to the content of the reframe but also to the approach of reframing itself. Message from God: stop! And try something else, before losing rapport further. See Reframe-Free Reframes – Chapter 10.

- when SUDS levels are too high – a reframe attempted when your client is 8 or more could be perceived by your client as your lack of appreciation or insight into their emotional state, and can be a major rapport-breaker. Apply some basic EFT or other therapy to reduce SUDS a little before continuing further.

- When insufficient rapport, too early in the therapeutic relationship.

- When client is completely dissociated – as you know, the whole therapy process concerns maintaining the client in a delicate emotional balance, emotionally associated enough that your therapy has a chance to work, but dissociated enough to prevent completely re-traumatising your client. At the same time, attempting to assist a completely "unfeeling" client using cold reframing is a poor use of their time and yours. Instead, with these sorts of folks, use something else, e.g. picture or visual or submodality techniques[1] to pull them enough into a memory as to get SUDS up and give your reframes some room to move.

Of course, ultimately it is your intuition and experience which will guide you in deciding if the reframe is right for this particular client, for this particular issue, at this particular moment.

Above all, your congruent delivery of the reframe to your client is often the deciding factor on its success – so, go with your gut instincts at all times, as even the finest of reframes will stray wildly off target if your client picks up on your lack of internal agreement with it. More about this in the next chapter - How To Deliver Reframes.

# ~ 4 ~

# How To Deliver Reframes

As you may have gathered, there is an art to delivering reframes. In this chapter, I'd like to share some of the ways of delivering reframes that I've noticed have increased my hit-rate dramatically. This includes aspects of delivery generally, as well as during the specific moment of delivering the reframe. Then I want to offer you a suggested pattern to delivering the reframes, an "anatomy of a reframe," if you will.

## *Association*

In my experience, getting the client associated into the problem situation, as it happened "back then," whilst the reframe is delivered, gets best results. It allows a maximum possible shift in the underlying belief and a maximum

Aha for the client. To do this, have the client talk about the event as if it's happening again now. Specifically;

- Use associated language – e.g. "this"; "here"; "in front of you"

- Use present tense language – e.g. "as you're see*ing* this *now*"; "at this moment"; "as you feel it now"; "As I look at him now, I am realis*ing* that…"

- Lead client into all representational systems of the situation – e.g. "feeling these feelings, and seeing him making those sounds in front of you now, what do you think about this situation?"

Use your detailed calibration skills very closely throughout the process.

## *Minimising Abreactions*

But, having said that, there is always a fine line to travel on, of keeping your client out of fight/flight, yet still in the experience enough to collapse it. So, the proviso on associating your client in the experience is to take the edge off any extreme intensity first.

I suggest a stuck SUDS of 6 or lower is a good starting level to be aiming your reframe at. Anything higher needs a few rounds of basic EFT first to bring your client to a manageable emotional state. This is important since, for best results, you will be inviting your client progressively more "into" the situation, and you need to minimise the risk of abreaction at all times.

For those who prefer a more specific procedure on how to deliver reframes, I offer the following.

## *Anatomy Of A Reframe*

1. **Establish the underlying emotion** - In my own work, I find the easiest route into reframing is to first establish the prevailing emotion the client is in. Once identified, I can then select from my bank of new perspectives (Chapters 8 & 9) the most appropriate to the situation at hand. Establish the underlying emotion by asking questions like

   a. "…and what did this mean to you?"

   b. "what decision did you make about yourself and the world, as a result of this experience?"

   c. "what did you learn from this?..." and so on.

2. **Pre-softeners** – I usually soften my reframe with a few nicely chosen words immediately before, like:

   a. "…it might just be possible that…"

   b. "…perhaps…"

   c. "…maybe, in some ways,…"

   d. "…maybe some people would consider it that…"

    e.   "…who's to say that…"

    f.   "…someone else looking at it might think…"

3.  **Calibrate** – After the pre-softener, on a moment-to-moment basis, I will be looking to intuitively pick up on the client's unconscious feedback on how open they are to my words, and adjusting my language accordingly.

4.  **Reframe** – Delivery of the reframe itself using appropriate language, tonality, speed, etc as before.

5.  **Calibrate** – Again I am constantly calibrating the client's non-verbal feedback, this time as an indication of how I might soften a post-frame.

6.  **Post-softeners** – If I intuitively pick up *any* hesitation or lack of acceptance at all, I will immediately post-soften, using phrases like those below. Even if my reframe has not landed, this will at least allow me to maintain rapport going forward and work the issue from another angle.

    a.  …maybe"

    b.  …once upon a time"

    c.  …so the story goes"

    d.  …in the gospel according to…"

    e.  …so says [me/him/her, etc]…"

f.    …or at least I *want* to [repeat setup], but I'm not there yet…"

After post-softening, look for tail-enders. Listen closely to your client's words and observe their body language for the "Yes, but…" Where is the objection taking you? To what underlying belief?

Mapped out in practice, the process might work like this (client presents with migraine and explains own anger at her brother for acting violently, destroying possessions in fits of anger, and expecting family and others to accept his behaviour):

| | |
|---|---|
| **Establish underlying emotion** | **Me** – And him doing that makes you feel?... <br><br> **Client** – Massive frustration. He doesn't realise that it's not OK to just smash things up whenever he feels like it, just because *he* feels like it. |
| **Calibrate** | Client is flushing red in face |
| **Pre-softeners** | **Me** - OK…(KC) Even though… (pause to observe client) it's possible that someone else looking at this situation… |
| **Calibrate** | I see no observable changes in client so I go ahead with my reframe. |
| **Reframe** | **Me** - …might see something different…might see a boy with issues…trying to get love somehow… |
| **Calibrate** | I'm not observing any conscious or unconscious |

| | |
|---|---|
| | objections from client, but at the same time I am intuiting that something more is needed for client's full emotional relief. |
| **Reframe** | **Me -** ...some form of love – be it attention, or the space to moan, or whatever, he's trying to get love, in the only way he knows how... and who can blame him for that?... |
| **Calibrate** | Client breathing deeply, flushing gone |
| **Post-softeners** | **Me -** (now tapping round the points) "...he's doing what he can, the only ways he knows how...it's his stuff...it's all his stuff, and me taking it on doesn't do either of us any good.... maybe the best thing I can do...is love him from afar...and be an example for him, of peace, of love, and of acceptance... |
| **Calibrate** | (Overt calibration)<br><br>**Me –** take a few breaths...how's the headache?<br><br>**Client –** it's dissolving fast... |

## The Need To Understand

Remember, most folks are coming to us with an underlying *need* to understand. Their main complaint is "If only I *understood* why/what/where/how it happened..." They are seeking above all to make sense of the situation they face(d) within their map of the world and to rationalise it within that same map. The stress and emotions a typical client presents with can *only* be due to happenings that have taken place outside of their existing beliefs and thus they are in emotional conflict with, represented physiologically and emotionally by disturbed sleep, cold extremities, pre-occupied and obsessive thinking, and other symptoms. Clients are only too happy to listen to your more plausible, and potentially more comfortable, version of how things happened, if they feel it will ease the internal dis-alignment with their beliefs they are currently feeling.

## *Reframing v Leading*

NLP offers us pacing and leading. But with reframing, we pace and offer. Always remember that with our reframes we are offering clients another way, not leading them into a version of how it "should" be. Then, we sit back, and observe with neutrality and dis-investment whether it lands with them or not. Leading clients into *your* version of events, even if they buy it, will help them only in the short term, as they will realise over time that that version does not fit some part of their identity and the issue (or aspects of it) will resurface again for further treatment. *Anything* we try to force onto our clients is only ever a reflection of our needs and our unresolved issues deserving attention before we work with another. Show other options, but do not lead.

## *When Reframes Go Wrong*

I often tell the story of the time I worked with a wonderful girl called Sarah* (name changed for confidentiality). Together we were working on some "Dad issues". Her father had aggressive tendencies, and Sarah felt rejected by her father frequently and in different ways. We had established that Dad's intentions were probably loving, even though he had a funny way of showing it.

I began leading her into a setup:

**Me:** "...Even though my Dad is a real b****** in this situation...maybe I can love him..." (pause to let client repeat)

**Sarah:** "Oh my God I can't!..(Sarah is turning deep red and beginning to hyperventilate) I can't love him!...Oh my God I can't love my Dad..." (now sweating, struggling for air, full blown panic attack)

## *The Power Of A Pause*

Soon after using continuous tapping and some fresh air, Sarah came down and was able to relax and recover from the situation. I explained to her afterwards where I was going; my *full*, uninterrupted, setup was

"Even though my Dad is a real b****** in this situation, maybe I can love him *for what his intentions were*..."

which has quite a different feeling to it without the pause, and would have helped Sarah soften her vibration and allowed further rounds of EFT maximum headroom to relieve emotions.

So allow all of this to remind you again: delivery is a delicate art. And remember that aside from the actual content of your reframe, you must have enough rapport established that the client is even willing to go there with you, at all.

You will sense also if it is the right time in your therapy relationship with this person how much of a mental/emotional stretch you are asking of them to "go there" with you at this point. Respect the client's need to travel at their pace. If you attempt too many reframes too fast the client will let you know their lack of acceptance in no uncertain terms which you will see in their unconscious responses. Use your discretion and intuition accordingly.

And, remember that even when your reframe does not land, you are still pointed in the right direction the therapy needs to go in next. Observing the client, is there a level of discomfort with the reframe such that softening the language might help it land better? Or, is a completely new approach required, perhaps a different emotion has come up and now needs to be dealt with first.

## *Try Something Else*

Let me be the first to say that reframing is sometimes not the answer for your client. Sometimes they just need something else. Maybe you have already offered several reframes, none of which have landed. In which case your client may be building an immunity to your efforts, and likely, frustration about the process itself. Be quick to defuse such situations by tapping on whatever resistance is there and switching doors or techniques to something fresh. As EFT Master Jacqui Crooks observes[1], sometimes just fully acknowledging the resistance and allowing it to be, is enough to reframe it and help the client feel better about it. Indeed, accepting and owning and tapping on the resistance itself, is often the most effective route. More on this in Reframe-Free Reframes (Chapter 10).

# ~ 5 ~

# The Setup Is A Reframe (And Why It Works)

The EFT setup is the first and perhaps most important reframe of any session. The basic setup statement is said out loud whilst tapping the KC point or rubbing the sore spot. And it works very well, for very specific reasons. Understanding how and why this principal reframe helps to realign the energy polarities is a cornerstone learning and will change the way you practice.

## The EFT Setup

"Even though [problem], I deeply and completely accept myself."

## Meeting The Client Where They're At

The point of the setup is to have the client accept themselves (and therefore the problem too) using a suitably softened phrase that matches their current vibration, and therefore, will "land." To make progress at all, the client needs to accept the problem first; so by crafting a suitably softened statement to have them accept all of themselves, we automatically include acceptance of the problem as well, and therefore increase our likelihood of EFT's effectiveness.

Sometimes clients have difficulty stating that they deeply and completely accept themselves, so we can soften the phrase to something more acceptable for the client's current vibration, like:

> ...I *want* to accept myself..."

> ...I deeply and completely *respect* myself..."

> ...I can think about the *possibility* of considering maybe accepting myself...*at some point*"

## The Setup Helps Us "Own" The Problem And Overcome Resistant Parts Of Ourselves

Very often in life we are so used to part of us pushing our problem away, and resisting and rejecting those parts of ourselves we don't like, that simply accepting them can be enough of a reframe to allow us to open up to the EFT and allow it to have greatest benefit.

Sometimes we create resistance by our meta-level frustration, anger, or other feelings, *about* the problem, i.e. frustration that the problem itself exists. Again this will block us from fully experiencing the problem and therefore disallow EFT from helping us as we tap.

As a general rule, if you are pushing the problem away, and not allowing it to be what it is, then you are simply not tapping on anything! A good example here is with physical pain. We tend to resist pain and become frustrated when it persists, disowning it, pushing it away, and thus immediately blocking the effects of any EFT. This is taught in basic prenatal birthing classes, that becoming stressed about the pain only puts us further into fight/flight and causes even more pain. Only by accepting an issue *fully* will EFT be allowed to work optimally.

Part of the reason the basic setup and variations work is by allowing us to accept all of ourselves, *including* this issue, knowing that it won't kill us, we've been through worse and lived, and so on. Subsequent rounds of EFT can then optimally balance the energy system, giving you terrific, lasting results.

Other setups I've found useful for not "owning" the issue are:

- "Even though the problem will just be what it is anyway…why resist it?…it's not going to change what it is just because of how I feel about it…why resist it?…this *irresistible* issue…"

- "Even though this problem doesn't know how to be anything else, it is [name problem], yet I'm over here expecting it to be something it's not…"
- "Even though I don't accept this problem…but I do! …it's there, in my [name physical location of problem]…how can I deny that?..."
- "Even though it's not a cat, or a piece of tile, or a chair, it is what it is…it's [name problem] and I'm OK anyway, with or without it…"

You'll find more in Chapter 9.

## NeuroLogical Levels

Another way to explain why the setup works so well, is best illustrated by reference to the NeuroLogical Levels model, originally conceived by Robert Dilts and taught in NLP(Neuro Linguistic Programming).

- NeuroLogical Levels
  - Spiritual/Greater System – Who else
  - Identity – Who I am
  - Beliefs/Values – Why
  - Capability – How
  - Behaviour – What
  - Environment – When, where, with whom

From bottom to top;

The environment level of experience is concerned with when, where and with whom we have the experience in question. For example, you are reading this book at the current time in your locale, in the place you are in, with the people who are around you.

The behaviour level is concerned with what actions you're doing in that environment. It is the level of behaviour-reinforcing techniques seen on *Supernanny* TV programs, and so on, and the realm of the majority of the anchoring techniques found in NLP. A change at this level might involve positively reinforcing a child after desirable behaviour with a view to having them repeat it again in the future.

The capability level looks at the how, i.e. what cognitive strategies do you use to do those behaviours in that environment? Classical NLPers make changes at this level by working with the modalities and sub-modalities of behavioural steps, and interrupting them and replacing them for better end results. Often this is anchoring and language work.

The beliefs/values level looks at why you do the strategies you do, to do those behaviours, in that environment.

The identity level deals with the results of all those beliefs – who I am.

And finally the spiritual level, deals with others outside our own physical bodies – who or what else might benefit from the results of my identity, beliefs, behaviours, actions, etc?

During therapy generally, the NeuroLogical Levels are useful as a way to keep track of where therapy is, and as a pointer to work on any levels of the problem you have not directly worked with.

## Why The Setup Works In Terms Of The NeuroLogical Levels

For our purposes, the EFT setup statement works because it is operating so high up the NeuroLogical Levels, at the identity level. When we state the setup, we are saying that despite all these problematic behaviours, beliefs, actions, and circumstances at the levels below identity, we accept ourselves, as a person, anyway, at the identity level. It is the highest level of acceptance we can offer ourselves, whilst in our physical bodies. When we accept ourselves at that level, all the levels beneath are automatically accepted in a cascade-down style. This is why, in my work, I am almost always looking to do belief therapy with my clients rather than behavioural or environmental therapy. I use the current emotions as a doorway to the underlying belief, applying EFT at that level for maximum benefit, throughout a person's life. And usually, when enough beliefs are changed, identity follows suit.

To do this, work on specific memories, then come back and check for the truthfulness of the associated belief using the VOC (validity of cognition) scale, e.g. after successful work on a memory containing embarrassment, checking the associated belief that "I can't put myself out there" by asking the client to state it out loud and rate how truthful it feels on a scale of 0-10. Importantly, you are looking for how true it feels *emotionally*, not logically.

However, I digress. The setup works as it reframes whatever blocks are present on the lower logical levels as acceptable anyway, regardless, no matter what. In other words, we make it *safe* for the person to connect with, and own, the problem they were previously pushing away. With this level of acceptance of the problem at hand, EFT now has a clear route to have full healing effect. Different softeners or rambling setups which achieve the same end will have the same effect, but the standard setup is a great place to start.

For a slightly different approach to a stubborn lack of self-acceptance, try alternate tapping on each point, between the problem and self-acceptance, e.g.

(TH) "[this problem]"

(EB) "I deeply and profoundly love and accept myself *without judgement*"

(SE) "[this problem]"

and so on.

I like to gently foster the energy into movement by sandwiching this between 3 rounds like this:

**1st Round:**

"I deeply and profoundly love and accept myself *without judgement*"

EVERY POINT


**2nd Round:**

(TH) "[this problem]"

(EB) "I deeply and profoundly love and accept myself *without judgement*"

(SE) "[this problem]"

and so on, ALTERNATELY


**3rd Round:**

"[this problem]"

EVERY POINT


*Always* calibrate yourself or your client *very* closely when repeating the setup, looking for any signs of incongruence, no matter how small, and adjust or soften your wording accordingly. A well timed and well phrased setup, properly delivered, can also aid rapport tremendously and act as a springboard for further cognitive shifts.

# ~ 6 ~

# My Top 5 Reframes & Why

## *Favourite Reframe Using Time*

One of my favourite reframes juxtaposes two moments in time together, to achieve a linguistic collapse of an issue. Full credit to EFT Master Tania Prince[1] for this one.

Assuming you are working with the client associated IN a specific event and are using present tense language, visual association, in mid-flow, with the client's attention in the memory "back-then", quickly ask the client a question which brings their focus back to the adult version of them, then quickly change back again into being back-then. For example, Tania working with a client, Carmen(not her real name), on fear she experienced at three years old, upon realising her parents had gone out, leaving her alone:

**"Karate Point:** "Even though I was three years old and no one was there, I am all alone, I completely and totally love and approve of myself"

**Karate Point:** "Even though there was no one there and I was frightened, I completely and totally love and approve of myself"

**Karate Point:** "So even though they left me and no one was there, I completely and totally love and approve of myself".

**Eye Brow:** "I was all alone"

**Side of the eye:** "No one was there"

**Under the eye:** They'd gone, mummy and daddy were never coming back"

**Under the nose:** I switched tonality at this point and directly addressed the adult client and asked;

"How long was it before they did come back?"

She laughed and said, "I think it was a few minutes, not long"

**Chin:** Switching straight back to the tonality and tense I had used before I had asked the question, I continued, "I was all alone"

**Collarbone:** "They are never coming back"

The words that I am using here when saying, "I was all alone", reflect Carmen's 3 year old's point of view.

At this point we stopped as Carmen was now finding it highly amusing. She obviously had shifted her original emotions."

By doing this you are helping the client to collapse the two cognitive ideas mentally together, simultaneously, in the same way as a collapse-anchor pattern works to collapse two states together in NLP. It is a kind of "linguistic collapse belief" pattern, and the fact that it works two logical levels above the standard collapse-anchor NLP pattern (see Chapter 5) makes it extremely powerful.

The client is able to fully experience the contrasting beliefs of the two moments in time, purely by making huge leaps in time along their timeline, in a few moments.

Speed is the key to this pattern, and therefore maximum rapport is of utmost importance as you will be leading the client in and out of very different belief-states within a few moments (the faster the better) for maximum results.

### Favourite Humour Reframe

"…and even though, by thinking about it in this way, in a way, I'm trying to pole vault over a mouse turd…"

Of course every joke is a reframe and some well-timed humour can rattle the bolts loose of even the most traumatic issue. I love this reframe as it can pull a whole session back from the brink, or equally make a good session great. Tasteful humour, impeccably timed, is another factor separating the masters from the merely competent and can help make your therapy a pleasure for the client.

This particular reframe never fails to get a laugh and is so general it can be easily applied in virtually any session, across a range of emotional issues. To reframe using humour my preferred methods are:

- exaggerate to the ridiculous
- generalise/role-reversal
- apply to self (often with some light self-depreciation)

Sometimes I could combine all three, e.g.

"...of course my principles in this situation are the best principles...the ONLY principles... so says me...and of course the others in this situation should already know my principles...and it's not like I would need to sit them beforehand and explain what my expectations are in this situation...no no no they will just read my mind of course...(they're good that way)...and all of this is in the gospel according to me.....Amen!..."

## *Favourite Guilt/Taking Too Much Responsibility Reframe*

"...and even though, in this situation, I am assuming that this situation is just about me and [perpetrator], *in this moment*, I remind myself, that TO this situation, each person brings their past...their responses and abilities in the now moment are a result of all their past experiences, and how they reacted in this situation is a result of their past experiences, which are nothing to do with me…"

I've never had a client with whom this reframe has not landed, and it gives a new, extended, slant on the classic "they were doing the best they could", which for heavy trauma, many people simply can't absorb.

Most of us would probably say that with the heavy traumas we've experienced we are simply looking to *understand* why it happened, how it happened, and so on. And, to know, above all, that we are lovable despite this event. And this reframe does exactly that; - it allows the client greater understanding whilst at the same time absolving their own responsibility for the event, that they may have been carrying.

The icing is the nice linguistic presupposition "I remind myself", which encourages the client to confirm internally that they knew this slant on things all along, that they had just forgotten, etc, and helps to strengthen the new understanding.

In my experience this is an extremely powerful reframe and deserves a place at the top of your therapy toolkit.

### *Favourite One-Size-Fits-All Reframe*

"...*people* [can achieve desired goal/can resolve relevant emotional issue/deserve desired goal etc].... *I* am a person, ...*I* [can achieve desired goal/can resolve relevant emotional issue/deserve desired goal... etc]"

This is as universal as it gets, and yet in my experience this one lands nearly every time, and is very hard to argue with, even for the most logical of clients. To deny this is to deny we are all worthy of achieving our desires, which few will do. In an NLP explanation, this is an "apply to self" reframe, and is the truest expression possible of treating yourself with the same love, respect, deservingness etc that you extend to others.

Accordingly, my favourite usage is in the sense of deservingness, e.g.

"*People* are lovable, they deserve to be loved, even after an event like this....*I* am a person...*I* am lovable..."

Again you can adapt this to almost anything and for me this is a great fallback reframe when the idea of self-acceptance is just not on the client's radar (yet).

### Favourite Reframe-Free Reframe

Reframing's objective is a change of perspective and my favourite reframe-free reframe does just that, without the verbals.

For those clients who are less cognitive, linguistic, etc simply changing perspective in a more visual way in the imagination can offer huge shifts in understanding the traumatic situation and help them move toward forgiveness of self and others. The key to this next method is to lead your client *fully* into the state and persona of each participant in the event as vividly as possible, and your language should reflect this.

I use an adapted version of the NLP change perceptual positions pattern. Here it is:

- Establish first what beliefs/decisions the client currently holds about the event, it's meaning, what the client has concluded about self and the world as a result of this event.
- Have client float in to each player's body in turn, describing from each perspective their beliefs and perception about the situation.
- Have client give perpetrator a piece of their mind, whilst you (gently) tap round the points. Can be done out loud or inside.
- Have client explain to perpetrator what they need in this situation.
- Have client explain situation to younger them then, helping young version of self make sense of what's happening, and filling in any knowledge gaps/answering any question young client has.

- Have the client give the perpetrator(s) the resources they need to behave differently, or to have the event turn out better for the client.

- In the same way, have the client give young self and any remaining others the resources they need to behave differently or have the situation turn out differently.

- Calibrate here. Check that the client and all players have *all* the resources they need to have the event turn out differently. Cycle back through giving and receiving of resources until client is completely happy to have event turn out differently. This is also an ideal time to assist your client with further reframes of the situation if necessary.

- Have the client now play out the event differently, in this new way, with each participant now having all they need to behave better.

- Check what decisions the client has now about the meaning of the event – what does the event mean now in terms of both the world and themselves? If necessary, recycle back through any steps of reframing or providing resources etc, until meaning has changed.

- Be sure to take the realisations and reframes up the timeline to the present day.

Many times in my own work this has been a powerful, pivotal point in the therapy, providing substantial relief on the heaviest of traumas. It is a comprehensive, powerful version of an already effective technique, and at the least will reduce SUDS to a manageable level or give new insights and directions to take the therapy next.

# Part 2: The Reframes

# ~ 7 ~

# The Emotional Levels Of Therapy™

As seasoned therapists we are well aware that many different flavours of the same emotion exist, but feel energetically different, e.g. anxiety is in the same family of emotions as worried or scared, but all three feel energetically distinct from each other. Many times it is only by resolving these very specific emotional flavours of a situation that we will *fully* clear an issue, and avoid future re-triggering.

During the course of my therapy work I arrived at a list of emotions and related emotional aspects that we all typically experience during trauma.

Having the list all in one place at one time, I found it particularly helpful to use when the client couldn't explain what they were experiencing internally; when my intuition was off the boil; or when, together, we just weren't hitting the target. It's also useful for those just starting out in this field. I've called it *The Emotional Levels Of Therapy*™.

The Emotional Levels Of Therapy™ (ELT) can be used as a general therapy tool; a tool to get to core beliefs; and more; but its primary use is as a reframing tool. I explain each below.

In table form, the ELT allows you to cross-reference the 'same-but-different' emotions your client might be experiencing, together with some suggested beliefs that may be driving them. In this way, using your client's current emotions, you have a quick reference point for several related emotional aspects to treat for, as well as the related table-top beliefs to reframe.

It's a very useful navigational tool and can be used from the perspective of working "inside" a specific memory, or just deciding where to take the therapy next.

The ELT is based on the excellent work of John Gray[1]. The first page of the ELT is the summary table, which groups together a summary list of all the negative emotions we commonly experience, together with the underlying blocks and beliefs. This page is used as a starting point, to correlate your client's presenting emotion with likely related emotions, underlying beliefs, and even tapping points to focus on.

It shows a menu of 12 negative emotions, split into 4 "families". Within each family are "the same but different" emotions e.g. family 1 is anger, frustration and resentment. Family 2 is sadness, disappointment, and hurt, and so on.

Thereafter, each of the 12 negative emotions has its own list of related *aspects* to tap for, i.e. a list of multiple language ideas for finding different aspects of the emotion to help the client hit the emotional bull's-eye. Applying EFT in this way, having found just the right expression of the emotion, gets maximum results.

## The Emotional Levels Of Therapy™

| Family | Block | Emotion | Possible Beliefs | Tapping Points |
|---|---|---|---|---|
| 1 | Blame Judgement Resentful | Angry Frustrated Envious | "People are untrustworthy" "People will let me down" "People will hurt me" | EB, SE, IF, MF, LF |
| 2 | Depression Indecision Self-Pity | Sad Disappointed Hurt | "I'm bad" "I'm broken" "I'm unlovable" | TH, MF, RF, LF |
| 3 | Anxiety Procrastination Confusion | Afraid Worried Scared | "The world is a dangerous place" "The world is cruel and unloving" "Always be on guard" | UE, CH, CB, UA |
| 4 | Indifference Perfectionism Guilt | Sorry Embarrassed Ashamed | "God is out to get me" "God can't love me" "I deserve to be punished" | UN, CH, IF, MF, KC |

## 1. Angry

Recall a time when you felt betrayed in some way

Recall a time when someone mistreated you

Recall a time when someone lied to you

Recall a time when someone disappointed you

Recall a time when someone opposed you

Recall a time when someone tricked you

Recall a time when someone ganged up against you

Recall a time when someone defeated you

Recall a time when someone turned on you

Recall a time when someone excluded you

Recall a time when someone rejected you

Recall a time when someone misunderstood you

Recall a time when someone criticised you

Recall a time when someone didn't keep a promise

Recall a time when someone talked about you

## 2. Frustrated

Recall a time when you felt dissatisfied in some way

Recall a time when you didn't get what you wanted

Recall a time when what you received was not what you wanted

Recall a time when others didn't measure up to your expectations

Recall a time when you didn't win something

Recall a time when you didn't do well

Recall a time when someone let you down

Recall a time when you were not progressing fast enough

Recall a time when you had to wait for someone

Recall a time when you didn't like someone

Recall a time when you didn't like a situation

Recall a time when you heard bad news

## 3. Envious/Deprived

Recall a time when you felt deprived in some way

Recall a time when you had less than others

Recall a time when you didn't get what you wanted

Recall a time when someone else got what you wanted

Recall a time when your sibling got more than you

Recall a time when you were ignored

Recall a time when you were neglected

Recall a time when you were not forgiven

Recall a time when you were punished

Recall a time when you didn't get to go

Recall a time when life was unfair

Recall a time when you did something nice and were then mistreated

Recall a time when something was taken from you

Recall a time when you didn't get to have your turn

Recall a time when someone had more than you

Recall a time when someone did better by cheating

Recall a time when someone cut in front of you

Recall a time when you got in trouble and it wasn't your fault

## 4. Sad

Recall a time when you felt abandoned in some way

Recall a time when you were left behind

Recall a time when you were unhappy

Recall a time when you were left alone

Recall a time when you were lost

Recall a time when you were rejected

Recall a time when you were left out

Recall a time when you were not picked

Recall a time when you were not missed

Recall a time when you were forgotten

Recall a time when someone was late

Recall a time when someone left

Recall a time when someone else got all the attention

Recall a time when you were less popular

Recall a time when someone disappointed you

Recall a time when you experienced failure or defeat

## 5. Disappointed

Recall a time when you felt discouraged in some way

Recall a time when you were disappointed

Recall a time when you didn't hear what you expected to hear

Recall a time when you didn't get to do what you wanted to do

Recall a time when you were going to do something and it was cancelled

Recall a time when you were not as good as you thought

Recall a time when you were less than others

Recall a time when you had less than others

Recall a time when you got less than others

Recall a time when you made a decision and it didn't turn out well

Recall a time when you made a choice and ended up missing out in some way

Recall a time when you were held back

Recall a time when you were grounded

Recall a time when you were a disappointment to others

Recall a time when you got in trouble

## 6. Hurt

Recall a time when you felt excluded in some way

Recall a time when you were left behind

Recall a time when you were rejected

Recall a time when you didn't get to go

Recall a time when you were left out

Recall a time when you were not invited

Recall a time when you were laughed at

Recall a time when you were mistreated

Recall a time when you missed out

Recall a time when you didn't get somewhere on time

Recall a time when others had a good time and you didn't

Recall a time when you were misunderstood

Recall a time when you were ignored

Recall a time when you were not allowed in

Recall a time when you were not dressed appropriately

Recall a time when you were different

Recall a time when you were judged by your skin colour, size, sex, or family

Recall a time when you did poorly on a test

Recall a time when others were jealous of you

## 7. Afraid

Recall a time when you felt uncertain in some way

Recall a time when you didn't know what to say

Recall a time when you didn't know what would happen

Recall a time when you were waiting a long time

Recall a time when you were held back

Recall a time when you were lost

Recall a time when you didn't know the time

Recall a time when you couldn't get home

Recall a time when you couldn't get water or food

Recall a time when you couldn't find your way

Recall a time when you ran away from danger

Recall a time when you needed help

Recall a time when you were waiting to find out a punishment

Recall a time when you didn't know what you did wrong

Recall a time when you didn't know how to protect yourself

Recall a time when you didn't know how to solve a

problem

## 8. Worried

Recall a time when you felt helpless in some way

Recall a time when you were little and needed help

Recall a time when you were lost and asked for help

Recall a time when you didn't know how to get home

Recall a time when you were new and didn't know how things worked

Recall a time when you couldn't make something work

Recall a time when you couldn't do what was expected of you

Recall a time when you felt pressured

Recall a time when you were late

Recall a time when you waited until the last minute

Recall a time when you finally got help

Recall a time when you eventually reached a goal

Recall a time when you struggled to get out

Recall a time when you were physically held back in some way

Recall a time when you didn't know whom you could trust

## 9. Scared

Recall a time when you felt hopeless in some way

Recall a time when you felt you didn't know what to do

Recall a time when you were late

Recall a time when someone you needed left or died

Recall a time when you were unable to do something

Recall a time when you didn't do something well

Recall a time when you were not as good as others

Recall a time when you couldn't make up your mind

Recall a time when you didn't have enough information

Recall a time when you didn't have enough help

Recall a time when you got mixed messages

Recall a time when you didn't know why you were punished

Recall a time when you didn't know why you were hurt in some way

Recall a time when you didn't know how to get out of something

Recall a time when you were chased

## 10. Sorry

Recall a time when you felt powerless in some way

Recall a time when you couldn't get what you needed

Recall a time when you couldn't please someone

Recall a time when you couldn't fix something you broke

Recall a time when you made a mistake

Recall a time when you couldn't undo a mistake

Recall a time when you couldn't do better

Recall a time when you didn't meet your expectations

Recall a time when you couldn't go somewhere

Recall a time when you could not do something

Recall a time when you were not accepted by others

## 11. Embarrassed

Recall a time when you felt inadequate in some way

Recall a time when you disappointed a parent or someone else whom you loved

Recall a time when others laughed at you

Recall a time when you said the wrong thing

Recall a time when you got into trouble

Recall a time when someone else got into trouble and you felt bad

Recall a time when you couldn't stop someone else from doing the wrong thing

Recall a time when you witnessed violence or abuse

Recall a time when you had more than others

Recall a time when your zipper was down

Recall a time when you publicly embarrassed yourself

Recall a time when you were someplace and you didn't know anyone

Recall a time when you were not picked

Recall a time when you were rejected

Recall a time when you failed

Recall a time when you had a big spot on your nose

## 12. Ashamed

Recall a time when you felt unworthy in some way

Recall a time when you were misbehaving

Recall a time when you were not helpful

Recall a time when you were not what others thought of you

Recall a time when you were not good enough in some way

Recall a time when you let others down

Recall a time when your body was not big enough or was too big

Recall a time when you realised something about your body was flawed or imperfect

Recall a time when something happened that had to be kept secret

Recall a time when you couldn't talk about something

Recall a time when you couldn't tell your mother

Recall a time when you couldn't tell your father

Recall a time when you couldn't stop something

Recall a time when you didn't measure up to someone's expectations

Recall a time when you couldn't tell the truth

Recall a time when you were inappropriate

Recall a time when you made a mistake

Recall a time when you upset someone

Recall a time when you felt you had more than others

Recall a time when you kept someone waiting

Recall a time when you felt different

## *How To Use It As A Reframing Tool:*

So, using the ELT, when the client presents with a certain emotion, you may easily correlate it to one of the 4 families and then refer to the most appropriate category of reframes in Chapters 8-9, which may suit, e.g. client presents with disappointment that he was not invited to a football game his Dad and brother were going to. Within this, there are two possible angles to reframe on; − if the aspect is (e.g.) frustration about perceived selfishness, then we could be reframing from Family 1 − anger, frustration, resentment. If the aspect is simply a 'purer' version of sadness about the issue, then we could be reframing from Family 2 − sadness, disappointment and hurt.

Continue asking gentle questions of your client until you're clearer which aspect it is the client feels most intensely. If it's not clear, or the client can't articulate it, prompt him/her with some example emotional aspects from the ELT lists, and calibrate closely for a response.

Once you've found the aspect that hit's the emotional bulls eye, you can now choose a reframe from that family, in chapters 8 or 9, to suit.

Using the ELT to cross-reference emotions in this way helps you cover more aspects, more accurately, and more thoroughly collapse issues. In short, you do a better job, faster. Like anything else, after you've used it a dozen or so times, it becomes automatic.

Sometimes some further clarification is needed with the client to understand the specific aspect they feel, but as a generalisation I have never been unable to retrofit an emotional complaint back to a well-targeted reframe using this method. Usually, clients will cycle through at least one emotion from each family before achieving full emotional release on a trauma.

## *How To Use It As A General Therapy Tool:*

• For *Complete* Relief From Stubborn Memories

Where your client's intensity refuses to shift, unresolved aspects are often at work. Establish what emotional 'family' the emotion the client is experiencing belongs to, then cycle through the language suggestions of the related emotions to find the aspect that hits the bull's-eye. Now you have a specific angle to begin tapping on.

• As A Starting Point To Find Unresolved Memories

Invite the client into a relaxed state using tapping, heart-breathing etc (http://www.stressreliefclinic.co.uk/Instant_Stress_Relief.html) or your preferred relaxation technique, then invite them to backtrack in their mind to relevant memories using the list of emotional aspects as prompts. Most will quickly find a relevant picture that 'comes up and meets them.' Very useful for helping "unfeeling" clients who claim they have *never* experienced any emotion, ever.

• For Use With Turbo-Tapping

Turbo tapping[2] is an extremely useful way to resolve many aspects at once, using EFT. It involves tapping on a different emotional aspect, very quickly, on each point. Refer to the original article (http://www.emofree.com/articles/turbo-tapping.htm) for a full explanation.

To use it with the ELT, use the suggestions under each emotional heading, tapping round the points using a different aspect on each point, to help the client resolve hidden layers of emotion. In this way the ELT provides you with a multitude of emotional aspects to collapse very quickly, all at once, in a few rounds. Calibrate your client closely throughout to see which ones land.

For example:

Client presents with frustration at friend's behaviour, and her own self-anger for reacting in the way she does.

**Client** – I'm just so frustrated that his doing this makes me feel this way again…

**Therapist** – You mean like…I'm more angry at myself than him?

**C** – (client flushes red) Yeah, I guess so…

T – Oh, OK... Even though he's done it again, I realise it's foolhardy to hold on to anger at him, he's just being him, he doesn't know how to be anyone else, and I now realise, that self-blame…is no better than blaming him…

From this dialogue I'm aware of two different emotions – anger at friend and anger at self. Using the table to cross reference I make a start on the client's outward anger, using the turbo-tapping list under number 3 – Envious/Deprived:

(TH) - I feel like he's got what he wanted

(EB) – I feel like he's got more than me

(SE) – Like I'm neglected somehow

(UE) – I'm the victim here

(UN) – It's not fair

(CH) – I do my best, and then I get mistreated

(CB) – My freedom's been taken from me

(UA) – I'm not getting to feel what I want to feel

(WR) – It's like he's doing better by cheating

(TH) – But blaming me instead of him isn't any better…

I would next repeat the turbo-tapping process using the list under 12 – Ashamed.

By doing this, in just two rounds you've had the opportunity to clear multiple relevant aspects. From here your client will tell you which 'feels' strongest to continue working on.

• For Assured Completeness And Testing Your Work

As you know, EFT is very big on testing your work, and using the list as a framework for working through layers of emotions will help ensure *all* angles of an issue are collapsed. I often find clients will work through the four layers of anger, sadness, fear, and guilt, in that order, before finding *full* release on an issue. Using the ELT you have more than enough variations in language at hand to resolve your client's specific emotional flavour of all such emotions.

## *How To Use It To Get To Core Beliefs:*

As a generalisation, to be experiencing unwanted emotions at all, the client HAS to be operating from an un-useful belief, which they know at their core, is inconsistent with their true, inner self.

For example:

- I am angry when I believe something else *should* have happened

- I am sad when I believe I don't matter, I am alone, or I don't make a difference or I don't count
- I am afraid when I believe I've done something wrong and may be punished
- I am sorry when I believe I did not uphold my values

And so on.

So the Emotional Levels of Therapy™ contains some related beliefs to look for, that the client may be operating out of.

## Why It's Useful To Work With Beliefs

Consider the classic NLP reframing question, "What would happen if you did?" For me, I understand the purpose of the question, but in a therapeutic situation I have seen it hit a brick wall many times. After cycling through the question several times, the client often becomes frustrated, e.g.

Client presents with burning desire to be the first to complete a project, in competition with peers:

**Therapist** – What would happen if you weren't the first?

**Client** – If I'm not the first I'm not going to get that head start in front of everyone else.

**T** – So what would happen if you weren't? Really?

**C** – What would happen if I wasn't?

**T** – Seriously, really consider, what would happen if you weren't the first?

**C** – I'd be the second or third.

**T** – And what would happen if you weren't the second or third?

**C** – Well eventually it would go on until I was the eleventh.

**T** – What would happen if you weren't the eleventh?

**C** – Well I wouldn't be.

**T** – No, I want you to fully consider, what would happen if you just weren't?

**C** – I would lose the advantage, and all of the effort I'd put in to it.

**T** – What would happen if you lost that advantage?

**C** – I'd be back with the pack.

**T** – And what would happen if you were back with the pack?

**C** – Then life becomes hard.

**T** – What would happen if life becomes hard?

**C** – Where did we get to…I'm lost…what's the right answer?…

**T** – No no no…what would happen if it was hard?

**C** – It would make my life harder…I'm not good enough…I don't know.

**T** – And what would happen if you weren't good enough?

**C** – Life would be difficult.

**T** – And what would happen if life was difficult?

C – I don't know...I can't get past this...I don't know where to go from there...

For me, a much more useful question is "how would you *feel* if it did?" Since this gets to the core *emotional* presentation almost immediately.

Why do we want to get to the core emotional presentation as quickly as possible? As a generalisation, in a therapeutic scenario, I am looking to find out, "what is the underlying emotion the client experiences most regarding this problem, and, (even more important), what belief is underneath that?"

Using the ELT, observe the suggested beliefs related to the emotion your client is experiencing most. Then, without putting words in his/her mouth, ask what belief they could be holding about themselves, life, etc along those lines.

Measuring the VOC (validity of cognition) scale of the belief, then you can begin looking for specific events to collapse that historically told your client this belief was true. How do they know the belief is true? If we were in a court and had to indict evidentiary experiences that told them this was true, what would they be? Once a few specific events have been collapsed, go back to the belief, measure the VOC again, and notice the difference. Much more useful.

It has always amazed me as to the lack of information available on specific models of therapy out there, and how to navigate a session successfully, and this is a very simple, highly effective one, perfect for use with EFT.

## *Worthy of Note*

Again, whether you are using the ELT to reframe, or get to the core issue, the key is not to lead but to suggest, and allow the client to define exactly what beliefs and emotions they are experiencing. I don't apologise for repeating again that rapport is always of utmost importance, as is your intuitive judgement on your client's congruence with any suggestions you make as to the underlying emotion or belief at play.

# ~ 8 ~

# Reframes For Anger, Sadness, Fear, & Sorrow

The reframes in this chapter cover all the emotions in the Emotional Levels Of Therapy tables, and this chapter should be your first call after you've identified what emotion your client is experiencing, and you need a reframe to apply.

Once again, I've split the reframes according to the four families of the ELT, for easy reference.

The reframes should be delivered using the format:

> **"Even though…[problem]…+…[reframe]…+…[self-acceptance]…+…[reminder phrase]"**

For example (where the reframe is in italics):

> Even though I can't forgive him, *it's an inside job, it's MY REACTION to what happened,* and I deeply and profoundly love and accept myself anyway…
>
> (TH) my inside job…
>
> (EB) my inside job…
>
> (SE) my reaction…etc

What follows below are the reframe portions only. If you've not yet done so, read the basic EFT protocol in the appendix now, to understand the EFT delivery.

In Chapter 9 I've provided a separate list of reframes, specifically for use in the self-acceptance part of the delivery.

Initially I wanted to split the reframes out into their component parts for you use, but doing so makes it difficult to give any one reframe the full meaning behind it. Just be aware that parts of these are intended to be interchangeable, so, like anything else, take the bits you can use and leave the rest.

## *Reframes For Anger, Frustration, Resentment (Family 1)*

The following reframes are useful when your client is experiencing emotions of anger, frustration, or resentment. You could be looking here for emotional blocks of blame, lack of forgiveness, jealousy, etc. Substitute your client's situation, names, perpetrators, etc into each and personalise as far as possible.

This phrase spoken whilst tapping the **Karate Chop** point.

### *Even though…*

1. they did [what they did]…they were just being [them] cos that's what [they] do…they don't know how to be anything else…

2. this issue is an inside job…it's not about what happened, it's about MY REACTION to what happened, it's my inside job, it's the writings on my walls, put there by someone else… …no-one else is doing this except me, and someone else seeing it might see something different…

3. I think I'm the best judge in the world of…

4. they did what they did…I forgive [perpetrator]…they're doing the best they can, given their background, beliefs, passengers

on their bus, and I'm doing the best I can, even though my background, beliefs, and training are different…

5. I can NEVER be angry enough to heal [problem]…

6. not even one tiny slice of my anger will change what happened in the past…

7. holding on to anger is like drinking poison then expecting the other person to die…

8. they were doing the best they could…even though it wasn't a very good best, in fact it was the worst best I've ever seen…it was still their best, given their baggage, beliefs, writing on their walls, etc…

9. by holding on to this anger I'm carrying a whole [perpetrator] with me wherever I go…I might just consider, possibly, forgiving them… at some point…

10. [perpetrator] had a lot of baggage, and (s)he passed it on to me…I'm going to pass it back…

11. [perpetrator] doesn't deserve to be forgiven, I don't deserve to carry all that around…

12. those messages were probably given with love, although it didn't feel like it at the time…

13. I'd rather be right than happy…look how clever I am!…

14. apparently they didn't know how to act around a [client's age then]-year-old. They didn't have the skills they needed. They didn't know how…

15. it might be the case, that one of my tasks here, is to understand the other person, because I now realise, that my anger only hurts one person, and that would be me…it's an inside job…

16. sometimes I think that if I'm REALLY angry, it'll somehow get to them, punish them, even though they're completely unaware of it and couldn't care less, and I'm over here all tied up about it…

17. I need to understand…but who could understand that?…sometimes everyone is doing the best they can…

18. it's not fair...it wasn't fair... fair is a matter of judgement, and it's my judgement here...and it's not fair that I have to carry this around...

19. ...and if it isn't fair...that means someone else probably thought it was fair, or it would never have happened...

20. this is my inside job....MY inside job, it's my response to what happened a long time ago, my response is my response, it's not THEIR response, it's MY response, and I have to live with it and carry it around... it's just not that helpful...

21. chances are, they were coming from a noble place, in their perception, whether or not I agree with it...

22. [incident] was unforgivable, unless you really get behind it... and understand how intense (s)he felt about [conflict content]..so whatever (s)he did, I can maybe understand where they were coming from...

23. part of me believes that I can be more in control if I'm angry, and it makes perfect sense, and I can be angry at George Bush and control him, and I wonder why the government hasn't hired me yet to control Osama Bin Laden...

24. I can control lots of things with my anger…I just wonder if I chose peace here, I might not need to…

25. this anger has cost me dearly, over decades… the only way I can really have peace here is to love them for what their intentions were…

26. anger is a curious thing…you have to be experiencing it yourself before you can send it out…so as long as you are angry, you are the one becoming the anger…you are both the target AND the recipient of your own anger…

27. I'm gonna sit here and be angry at [perpetrator]…I'll show him/her… I'll sit here and have all the vengeance in the world, I'll screw up my [list physical symptoms], I'll show him/her, you got it!!… vengeance is mine…revenge is sweet…vengeance is mine…I'll get you...you son of a...look how clever I am!…

28. I'm angry at him/her, I'm not gonna let it go, I'm not gonna let [perpetrator] have peace, cos they don't deserve it, and I'm not going to have peace, cos I'd rather have all these ailments, it's a lot more fun to have these ailments…I get to kick [perpetrator] around, but (s)he doesn't feel a thing, I forgive myself for all this anger at [perpetrator], for all these years...maybe it was

justified, maybe not, but it's costing me dearly, and maybe, just maybe, they were doing the best they could, truly...

29. sometimes I think that if I'm angry enough, (s)he'll change/it'll change what happened...change damn you change!...I'm beginning to wonder if me being angry is actually achieving anything at all...

30. by letting go of this anger I may be losing an old friend here...

31. there's an old Chinese proverb that says, "if you're going to seek revenge, you better dig 2 graves, cos you might get revenge, but it'll kill you in the process..." and I'd rather be dead and even than let this anger go!!!...

32. anger is like a snake bite... it's not the bite that kills you, it's the poison that continues to circulate in your system long after the bite has happened...and that's what I'm doing with this anger...

33. forgiving [perpetrator] is not saying what (s)he did was right, it's saying I'm not allowing them to influence the rest of my life....

34. they did [what they did]...they did what they thought they had to do...I have to accept them for what they did...I wouldn't want anyone to not accept me for what I do...I always have my reasons...right, wrong, or otherwise...

35. the thought that, in this situation (s)he had the extra mental resources, the capacity, the choice, to NOT do what they did, yet they still chose to do it anyway, DOES seem unlikely, now that I think about it...maybe they truly WERE doing the best they could...

36. they were just trying to get love in the only way they knew how...by the only means they had available...and who can blame them for that?...

37. they did what they did, I might choose to forgive them, not because they deserve to be forgiven, but because life is short, and precious...

38. they did what they did..it might just be possible... that (s)he was operating out of his/her own pain...

39. their judgements of me only reflect THEIR limitations... the limits and blocks they place on themselves... it's them that has to live with those limits, not me, I'm over here and I'm

fine...I'm just going to witness, and observe, how they limit themselves...

40. the situations of MY life until now have led me to the reactions I have in situations, my beliefs, my ways of being, and I can't be held responsible for all those events that got me here, likewise THEY'VE had their own experiences that led them to do what they did, in that situation, and I can't hold them responsible for all the experiences that got them to that place...

41. this is someone with big needs, with BIG needs...and no other way to get them...

42. this is where they've arrived at...this is their way of attempting to GET LOVE....it's their distorted attempt to get love, somehow, anyhow...somehow they've learned that this behaviour is a way to get love, or appreciation, or whatever, it's what they've arrived at...like a bully's only way to get attention is to bully...it's not by choice...it's not their preference...it's what they've been given, they're just trying to get love like everyone else...it's the only means they have...

## *Reframes For Sadness, Disappointment, Hurt (Family 2)*

The following reframes are useful when your client is experiencing emotions of sadness, disappointment, or hurt. You could be looking here for blocks of discouragement, depression, or self-pity. Again, substitute your client's situation, relevant names, etc into each reframe.

This phrase spoken whilst tapping the **Karate Chop** point.

### *Even though...*

1. I can NEVER be sad enough to heal [problem]...

2. I can NEVER be sad enough to change what happened...

3. this happened...people get through this sort of thing...I am a person, and I will get through this thing...

4. this happened, I was doing my best at it, and they didn't get it...that was THEIR limited thinking...

5. I've been through this trauma, and the challenges have probably in some ways helped me grow and become stronger, and helped me ultimately achieve what I've achieved...I

sometimes wonder if I'd ever have made these achievements if God didn't have this bigger plan for me…

6. this is God(or life) moving me, changing me into the person I need to be, by the only way he (or it) knows how…if I go to the gym, I need to stretch my muscles and push myself to grow, and this is no different…

7. I've gone through hell, it might just be possible that I've come out the other side knowing more about myself as a person…maybe I know more about myself and what I really want in life…maybe all this has, in some way, helped me to feel my wants and to come from that place…

8. I went through this, I wonder what I know now or realise now, as a result of going through this experience, that I didn't realise before?…

9. …I know now that circumstances do not make a man…they just reveal him…

10. I'm still reacting to little [client's name]'s response to [problem]…in a way I'm still taking the advice of that little person, and I wouldn't take advice from any other little person…

11. I have this [problem]…it's there for a reason… and the reason probably served me at some point, some time, some where, but I don't need it any more…I love and forgive myself, for anything I may have done to contribute to it, and I love and forgive anyone else who may have contributed to it…

12. sometimes I confuse this sadness with [secondary gain]…[Used in the sense where the client is getting some kind of positive reward (love, attention, etc) for doing the behaviour he wants to stop, hence the confusion and the realisation that it is not the behaviour he wants, but the love behind it]

13. [it] happened…I was just an actor on the stage at the time…[perpetrator] was the director, I had to do what [they] said…I don't have to anymore…

14. I have all these emotions about this…no matter what they are…it's a yesterday thing, it's as much in the past as falling off a bike…I was only [client's age then]…

15. it's not happening now, it's in the past, it's a fiction that it's happening now, I'm able to bring it up as if it was now, it's not here but I'm able to bring it up as though it was…

16. I'm disappointed they [had no reaction/reacted like that/didn't take an interest/they didn't get it/etc]...I could be feeling this way because my expectations were unrealistic...of course everyone should know what *my* expectations are...in fact I wonder if *anyone* else knows what the writing on my walls is?

17. I feel [left out/left behind/lost/etc]... maybe, within that, I'm jumping to the conclusion that where they're at, is somehow better or more valuable than where I'm at...and why should that be?...

18. I feel [sad/disappointed/hurt/left out/etc], it might just be possible, that others just can't recognise what I have to offer...I'm not responsible for the writing on their walls...it's *them* that has to carry that around, not me...

19. I'm so sad that I was [left out/left alone/left behind etc], maybe I'm assuming that they know how important it was to me...I guess they can't read my mind...

## Reframes For Fear, Worry, Scared (Family 3)

The following reframes are useful when your client is experiencing emotions of fear, worry, or scared. You could be looking here for blocks of anxiety, procrastination, or confusion. Substitute your client's situation, names, perpetrator, etc into each reframe.

This phrase spoken whilst tapping the **Karate Chop** point.

### Even though...

1. feeling confused means I am learning...means I have not yet decided, means I have an open mind...means I am growing...I'm not yet an expert...and I don't WANT to be an expert...A beginner has many, many options and choices and is willing to try ANY of them...an expert has pre-judged the whole thing and cuts himself off from many possible solutions...the worst thing you can be is an expert...…I let go of the need to be certain right now...some of the most beautiful things in the world take a long time to come in to being...I choose to not know YET...

2. [when client has no control over outcome in question] I don't have control over it, so worrying about it makes no sense...it's completely wasted energy...

3.  [when client does have control over outcome in question] I do have control over it, and I'm still worrying about it...which is insane really...by worrying about the future I'm denying my ability and pleasure to live in the present moment...

4.  [what client wants] COULD be happening, just not on my terms, or in the way I want, or at the time I want...

5.  [they/the world] will go ahead and do what it does anyway, with or without me worrying about it...someone on the other side of the world is probably doing something right now that I could get worried about...and I can't do anything about that...things will happen, people will do things, but over protecting myself like this is just not useful...I'm constricting and limiting myself...

6.  I'm hell-bent on controlling the world......I'm a megalomaniac...

7.  it/they is/are just going to be what they are...they don't know how to be anything else, yet I'm expecting them to be something different...it/they don't know about my expectations, they're just being them, innocently, not intending any harm...

8. I need (love/attention), we all need (love/attention), …sometimes I mistake (problem situation) for love [Used in the sense where the client is getting some kind of positive reward(love, attention etc) for doing the behaviour he wants to stop, hence the confusion and the realisation that it is not the behaviour he wants, but the love behind it]

9. I'm so arrogant as to believe I know what everything thinks/ is thinking………and if I was that powerful I would be hired by the President to tell what other countries are thinking, or by Microsoft, or…or…Or, on the other hand, I might not know what people think…

10. I can NEVER be afraid enough to heal [problem]…

11. I can NEVER be anxious enough to change what will happen…

12. this fear is like being drunk, it translates in my body as a drug, I'm seeing things exaggerated. I'm over-emphasising some things, I'm drunk...I'm drunk…

13. part of me is afraid about giving this up......I remind that part that it has the choice just to *be* after I've released this, I don't have to be, do, or say anything, I can just *be*...

14. I don't know who I'll be without [problem]...I'll still be me without it...

15. I've tapped on this fear and it's gone down... which means it's not even real, not even a real thing...

16. I don't even have a concrete reason to be afraid...like if I look out the window of the airplane and the engine's on fire...now THAT'S a reason to be afraid. but I don't have one of those...

17. I'm afraid because of these stories I making up/telling myself...

18. resolving my fear is actually the best gift I could give to those around me...

19. I'm a prisoner to the writing on someone else's walls...

20. it might be unsafe for me to let this problem go...I'm going to let it go anyway cos it's costing me dearly...

21. I have this [problem]...of course I'm the only one who's ever had a problem with [problem], no one else has ever had a problem with [problem]...

22. it could be risky not being a perfectionist, and making mistakes, it can't be that bad...after all, even a broken clock is right twice a day...

23. by thinking about it like this, I might just be crediting it with too much importance...after all, nothing is *that* important...

## Reframes For Sorrow, Embarrassment, Shame (Family 4)

The following reframes are useful when your client is experiencing emotions of sorrow, embarrassment, or guilt. You could be looking here for blocks of powerlessness, perfectionism, or guilt. Again, substitute your client's situation, relevant names, perpetrators, etc into the reframe.

This phrase spoken whilst tapping the **Karate Chop** point.

### *Even though...*

1. this event happened TO me ...and sometimes I think I am responsible for the events that happen to me, I remind myself that I am not responsible for the things that happen to me, they just happen...and I give up the need to know why they happen...

2. this happened, I was doing the best I could, after all, who gets out of bed in the morning saying "Hey! How can I really mess this day up?"...

3. I believe I am responsible for ALL this stuff, I must think I'm REALLY important...but there's another word for taking too much responsibility...it's called narcissism...

4. If I'm going to take responsibility for other people then I'll have to take responsibility for you and everything you do.... you do some pretty crazy s***... I sometimes wonder if I should be taking responsibility for all this other stuff too, for EVERYONE...

5. I always do the best I can with the resources I have available at that moment in time... I ALWAYS have good intentions...

6. this thing doesn't represent everything about me...it's not my entire person, it's not the last word on me...it doesn't represent me as a person...it doesn't describe all of me...there's much more to me...skills, abilities, resources, attributes, and I am ultimately innocent, and always worthy of love, and I always have good intentions...

7. I sometimes confuse responsibility with control, and control with responsibility....

8. this happened...people deserve good things in life...I am a person, and I deserve good things in life, and I deserve to feel good...anyway...

9. I don't feel good enough to [get outcome]...a person is going to [get this outcome]...and I am a person...

10. I'm so powerful I cause everything...including my own problems...it was there for a reason, and...I don't need the reason anymore...

11. I take responsibility for everything, all the natural disasters, all the accidents, tsunamis and government crises...

12. I have this [problem], the fact that I have allowed myself to live with this is ABSOLUTELY FINE...I forgive myself for doing that all this time...a part of me was doing it for a reason, for a good reason, that made sense at the time, it just doesn't anymore... and I choose to let it go...

13. I have this [problem], everyone has the same rights and worthiness and deservingness in this world ...we are not born any different, any more or any less ...I am worthy of love even WITH this problem...

14. I may be carrying this around for reasons that are totally illogical, that somehow I think served me some place else, some other time...maybe I get attention, maybe I get to moan, maybe whatever ...I deeply and completely accept myself for having all these needs, and I thank and honour all the parts of me for giving me these messages...

15. I think my problem is who I am, it defines me...and I confuse myself with my problem...I need to remind myself that who I am is much more than that...

16. I'm the [least/most/worst/best/biggest/smallest/world's greatest/world's worst/single-most/never/always] [problem]...or at least that's how it feels sometimes...

17. I'm going to die someday...I know that...the only question is, whether I'm going to allow myself to live first...

18. I DON'T forgive myself for this [problem]...I would never pin this on anyone else, and self-blame is no better than blaming someone else...

19. I can NEVER be sorry enough to heal [problem]...I deeply and completely accept myself, regardless...

20. I can NEVER be sorry enough to change what happened...

21. I never feel guilty that I am well, while others are sick...and I can never be hungry enough to feed one starving child, somehow I'm managing to feel guilty about this...somehow

I'm believing that this feeling bad is helping in some way...which does seem ridiculous...

22. I have to be perfect...and of course everyone loves a perfect person!...hands up everyone who loves perfect people...

23. I [did something] at age [client's age then], I didn't have many resources at age [client's age then]; who does? It was the best I could do...

24. I feel inadequate... from the judgement/comments/words of an inadequate man/woman...my inadequate feelings from a man/woman who felt inadequate themselves...

25. I have this notion, that somehow if I punish myself, and make myself feel bad, that somehow that'll improve what I'm doing or help me be better in some way, which doesn't really make sense now that I think about it...

26. ...I was born deserving, I'll die deserving....the only question is, if I'll give myself a break for the bit in the middle...

# ~ 9 ~

# Reframes For Self-Acceptance

The reframes in this chapter are alternatives to place within the self-acceptance part of the delivery. In my experience this is the part clients frequently struggle with, and the options provided here will give you more flexibility in helping overcome reversals of this nature.

The reframes should be delivered using the format:

> **"Even though…[problem]…+…[reframe]…+…[self-acceptance]…+…[reminder phrase]"**

For example (where the self-acceptance part is in italics):

Even though I can't forgive him, it's an inside job, it's MY REACTION to what happened, *and I deeply and profoundly love and accept myself anyway...*

(TH) my inside job...

(EB) my inside job...

(SE) my reaction...etc

What follows below are the self-acceptance portions only. If you've not yet done so, read the basic EFT protocol in the appendix now, to understand the EFT delivery.

## *Reframes For Self-Acceptance*

In my experience, the emotions associated with a lack of self-acceptance are usually from Family 4 of the ELT, so it's worth looking again at those reframes now, as well as these stand alone reframes. Many of these involve just small changes in the wording which can make all the difference with certain clients.

This phrase spoken whilst tapping the **Karate Chop** point.

## *Even though...*

1. I have [this problem], it's acceptable, I accept this version of me that has this [problem]. It's OK, it's forgivable, I'm human....I give myself permission to have this [problem]...

2. I have [this problem], I totally accept all of me now...

3. I have [this problem], it's only temporary, it's just the current version of me...it's not the last word on me...

4. I have [this problem], I totally love and accept this me now, even WITH this problem...I'm deserving, I'm worthy of love, I'm lovable, it's OK for me to have it...

5. I have [this problem]...I can love myself, even with this problem...

6. I have [this problem]...I accept myself WITH all my faults and failings...

7. I have [this problem]...I deeply and profoundly love myself JUST AS I AM...

8. I have [this problem]...I deeply and completely accept myself, REGARDLESS...

9. I have [this problem]...I deeply and completely accept myself/forgive myself/love myself WITHOUT JUDGEMENT...

10. I have [this problem]...I deeply and completely accept myself/forgive myself/love myself ANYWAY...

11. I have [this problem]...I accept myself WHILE I have this problem...

12. I have [this problem], I'm a good person, kind to animals, not myself!!...

13. I have [this problem]...I deeply and completely *respect* who I am...

14. I can't accept myself...I accept that I can't accept myself, and at least I can accept that I can't accept myself...

15. I can't accept myself...I'm deserving of love, no matter what happens...

16. I can't accept myself...I'm worthy of just being me...

17. I can't accept myself...I'm worthy of being true to my feelings...

18. I can't accept myself...*I'm* OK, no matter what the outcome...

19. I can't accept myself...I can forgive myself, no matter what the outcome...

20. I can never be (emotion) enough to give up my innocence/deservingness/right to...

21. I don't accept myself...I choose to relax, and just witness...

22. I'm not good enough, and I don't accept myself...what if I'm still acceptable?...

23. I'm not good enough, and I don't accept myself...what if I changed?...

24. I'm not good enough, and I don't accept myself...what if I am good enough?...

25. I'm not good enough, and I don't accept myself...what if I've been good enough all along?...

26. I'm not good enough, and I don't accept myself...I am enough right now...

27. I'm not good enough, and I don't accept myself...I appreciate who I am...

28. it's familiar and safe that I'm not good enough...I choose to accept all of me right now...

29. it's familiar and safe that I'm not good enough...I'm OK, with or without it...

30. I don't accept this [physical complaint]...I do!!... It's there!... in my [name physical location]...

31. I have this [problem]...I give myself complete and total permission, to heal myself now...

32. this is stuff that I don't even want to face...I let go of all my own contribution to it...

33. I have this [problem]…I forgive myself, for all the things this allows me to hide behind…I'm so comfortable hiding behind it, for so long…I'm ready to let it go now…

34. I have this [problem]…I allow myself to join the human race, and let it go…

35. part of me possibly thinks it's a good idea to hold on to this…the rest of me knows better…

36. at some point, part of me decided that "I will choose to hold on to [emotion experienced] before I ever experience [nature of trauma] ever again"… and so over time I'm locking myself out of my own feelings, and I'm paying the price…

37. I'm not acceptable, what if I misinterpreted that one event...

38. I'm not acceptable, what if I'm not really [underlying belief]…

39. I'm not acceptable, what if I'm OK, really...

40. sometimes I'll do anything to hold on to this [emotion] no matter what, no matter how big a fool it makes me look, no matter what the cost…

## ~ 10 ~

## Reframe-Free Reframes

By now you will have realised, that in reframing, we are simply overcoming the little parts objections the client has, along the path of the session, to help release *all* aspects of an issue.

In this chapter I would like to offer you some ideas and examples on overcoming objections *without* clever reframes, or wondering what you are going to say next.

Often I will use these within the first or second sessions with my client so that there is a clear line of sight thereafter straight through several traumas.

### *Bundle Together*

A very simple way to start is to have the client "bundle together" all the aspects of the objections into one round of tapping and tap on different aspects of the objections on different points, e.g.

(TH) "He doesn't deserve to be forgiven"

(EB) "It doesn't feel safe to let this go"

(SE) "I'm scared of this process"

(UE) "And of who I'll be if I get over this"

and so on.

After a few rounds you can begin argument tapping the willingness to let the issue go, e.g.

(TH) I want to let this go

(EB) No I don't

(SE) It's holding me back

(UE) It's keeping me safe

(UN) I'm not safe anyway

(CH) I want to let this go

(CB) But I'm not sure how

(UA) This problem is comfortable…it works!!!

(WR) I'll still be me without it….

and later you can introduce choice statements[1] to overcome any remaining objections or intensity.

Remember to check in frequently with your client to check SUDS levels throughout.

For me personally this has had a lower success rate generally, but where it is successful, it can clear multiple layers of objections *very* quickly. Be careful of activating too many dormant aspects and opening up cans of worms that will not clear quickly. Therefore I recommend using this approach with those for whom EFT already lands well, and are not otherwise already massively psychologically reversed.

## *Physicalise & Tap*

An extension of bundling together, this is about having the client immediately physicalise and tap on the resistance *as soon as* you notice SUDS levels are not going down. Having the client tap directly on the resistance, objections, or feelings *about* having this problem has many advantages.

First, by physicalising the issue, you are keeping the client body-focussed and therefore emotionally comfortable, and out of fight/flight. In this way it is a great way to minimise risk of abreaction with very intense issues.

Another advantage. Additionally, your energy as therapist is not affected by the content, and your client can retain their privacy over the detail of their issue. It's a win-win for all.

Also, by instructing the client to follow whatever the feeling changes to, you are very quickly and efficiently handling multiple emotional aspects quickly and comfortably, without the need to get involved. As yet another benefit, you are avoiding the sometimes challenging task of having the client successfully articulate exactly what aspects of resistance they feel, and how, which can be very difficult for most of us, and very time consuming in a clinic setting.

In this situation I would be tapping on the client and I would use a dialogue like this:

"Feel all the parts of you objecting to this in different ways and allow yourself to feel all your concerns re this situation, me, this process, any feelings *about* letting this go, and so on. Focus and concentrate intensely on this physical feeling and allow it to be...and when the feeling changes, that's absolutely fine, let it change and continue to focus on whatever it is..."

Likely you will do many (many) rounds of straight tapping with no verbalisation as the client feels and dissolves repeated layers of blocks.

Check back in with the client often for remaining aspects and physicalise those also, and repeat again. Be certain to take all aspects and objections down fully to zero before continuing.

Many times you will find by clearing objections together in this way you now have an open door to collapse multiple related memories with straight tapping *very* quickly and easily. Even just clearing the objection alone can provide a huge sense of relief and energetic shift for the client before tapping on any specific memories at all.

## *Metaphor*

Metaphor I see in the same way; i.e. as a quick way to get multiple aspects combined and ready for tapping on, together in one energetic "space", getting round the need for elucidating the detail. Except in this case we are having the unconscious/imagination translate all the aspects in milliseconds into another form other than the physical or emotional. Accordingly, this is one to use perhaps when SUDS are lower or more manageable, and you have confidence that no abreactions are likely.

The specific metaphor you use is limited only by your imagination and your intuition will guide you in the right direction based on the conflict content.

My favourites are animals, cars, pieces of music, colours etc, and often I will use something connected to an area I know my client has an interest in anyway.

Very simply, have the client describe the main player of the conflict in terms of the chosen metaphor. Then ask about the relationship between these players, in the third person,

e.g.

> Client presents with anger, resentment at the dentist whom she saw as incompetent, angry, and carrying out unnecessary and painful repeated treatment. Client feels she is being attacked by dentist and his assistant. We have already tapped several rounds for the anger without significant release…

> **Me** – So, giving me your first answer, as you think about this scene, if everyone in the scene were animals, what animals would they be?

> **Client** – An angry gorilla (dentist), a horse (the assistant), and a dog (client)

> **Me** – Good. So let's think about the gorilla. What's he like?

> **Client** – He's angry, his face is bright red, and he's jumping up and down on top of the dog.

> **Me** – What does the dog think about the gorilla?

**Client** – He's confused, and he looks angry. Looks like he doesn't understand why this is happening. Looks bewildered and scared. He thinks the gorilla is an oaf and clumsy, and he feels attacked.

**Me** – Good. And what about the horse? How does the horse relate to all of this?

**Client** – The horse is just an innocent bystander. Looks slightly confused.

**Me** – OK, so, Even though, this big red angry gorilla seems to be taking his anger out on the dog...I'm just gonna witness it.... (TH) that angry gorilla (EB) that angry red gorilla (SE) he doesn't know any better...etc etc


Keep the client talking in the third person throughout. Opening up this avenue alone will provide many angles for further work, in a way that is mostly content-free and emotionally comfortable for your client. The metaphor frame allows you to dissociate the client; gives an easy means to exaggerate to humorous effect, and combines many aspects in one energetic space for bulk tapping and resolution. Remember that you are using the metaphor as a door into relieving the resistance around the actual issue, and *not* the issue itself, so be sure to check back with the client on remaining feelings of resistance after a few rounds of EFT. Repeat the process on remaining aspects until full relief from resistance is experienced. Only when resistance is zero will you begin tapping on the actual issue itself. By using the metaphor, you are helping the client to express and relieve the aspects of resistance they cannot effectively verbalise in more specific rounds of tapping.

## *Free-Flow Tapping/Dialogue Tapping/Piece-of-My-Mind Tapping*

Sometimes the client's unconscious objection is simply due to the intensity or amount of unexpressed and unreleased emotions from the conflict situation. Having a framework or a few different ways to help the client release these is a good addition to your toolkit.


Here's how.


One way is to simply have the client imagine themselves in that situation, as if it's happening now, looking at the perpetrator, and have them rant, uncensored, whilst you gently tap on them to help the release.


Adapt this slightly and use it with specific events. Read more about this at http://www.stressreliefclinic.co.uk/Flow_Tapping.html


Choose this method only if SUDS are 6 or below, and you are intuitively certain of no risk of abreaction.


For clients who need more guidance through the process, try using the Emotional Levels Of Therapy™ table (Chapter 7) as a guide through the levels of release. I play Blankety-Blank with my clients and have them complete leading statements such as:

"I'm really angry at you because _____"

"I'm really sad about this because _____"

"I'm afraid that_____"

"I'm sorry that_____"

Naturally have your client contextualise these statements into the situation for maximum effect. Tapping through *all* levels and aspects attached to these statements in this way will help greatly to overcome the blocks towards release, and ultimately, forgiveness.

## Split-Screen Tapping

When the reasons and aspects of the client's resistance seem clear and are relatively few (three or less) sometimes a few rounds of split-screen tapping can clear enough of a path through. I love these silent tapping, no-verbals alternatives, as it clarifies for the client very quickly that it is in fact the tapping and energy work that is clearing these issues and not the language work alone.

It's like this.

Have the client picture a representation of the current issue they are trying to deal with, on the left hand side (or right if left-handed) of a split screen in their mind. This is the issue itself, *not* the feelings of resistance.

On the right hand side (or left if left-handed) have the client picture a representation of their resistance to getting over the issue (this can also be any secondary gain issue that is getting in the way that is not necessarily "resistance"). Their first picture is usually the best one.

Now, with the eyes closed and the client looking at these two pictures on the same screen at once, do several rounds of silent tapping (very gently, so as not to disturb client's focus). Afterwards, ask the client to notice how the pictures have changed in terms of their properties, size, colour, distance etc. Even if you have not completely resolved the pictures you will have some quality pointers to the underlying issues behind the resistance which you can now specifically address.

## Argument Picture Tapping

Split-screen tapping can be modified and used as an extension of Carol Look's wonderful back and forth style of argument tapping, using pictures.

Thusly. Again have the client picture a representation of the current issue, and another picture representing their resistance to letting the issue go.

Now simply have the client focus and silently tap on each picture, alternately, through the points, e.g.

(TH) client focussing on anger picture; tapping silently.

(EB) deep breath, client focussing on punishing Dad picture (as a reason not to let anger go); tapping silently.

(SE) client focusing on anger picture; tapping silently.

(UE) deep breath, client focussing on punishing Dad picture; tapping silently.

and so on.

Guide the client through the points and pictures *slowly* and gently, and ensure (s)he is fully engaged emotionally with each picture as you go.

Pushing together the states of the two pictures alternately, whilst working with the energy system simultaneously, usually achieves a very effective collapse of the issue.

## The Best Reframe Of All?

We can spend *a lot* of time helping clients overcome specific aspects of a situation. Sometimes they can explain the aspects to tap on; and sometimes we intuit what's going on, but we always validate and calibrate our tapping with the client along the way.

But what reframe will *always* be appropriate, requires minimal input from you, is always in the right language, requires no guesswork, and will always land with your client? Of course, one that's from them.

Once you've identified a traumatic memory that resists release, zero-in on the most traumatic aspect, and try this question:

"Take yourself back then to before this happened, and imagine you can see ahead in time and you know [this event/most traumatic aspect] is going to happen. What would you have needed to know to make it OK for [this event/most traumatic aspect] to happen?..."

Then, take your client's response and "tap it in" over a few rounds of EFT. Use their specific language throughout. Have them focus on all the emotional crescendos of the event, whilst tapping in these new realisations that help rationalise the event. Run through the event in this way as many times as it takes to ensure the entire incident is clear (SUDS zero).

Simple, elegant, and precise, this one question ensures that whatever reframe or rationalisation your client comes up with is already built around their model of the world, pre-existing beliefs, etc, and so will *always* land. A sure-fire winner.

# Part 3: Live Transcripts

## ~ 11 ~

# Live Transcript Of An EFT Reframing Session: Kathryn – Weight Issues

I'm lucky enough to have worked with Kathryn (name changed for confidentiality), a gentle and talented woman, looking to move closer to her ideal weight.

This was a single, one-off session, and you will notice the specific questions I ask that relate to the META-Medicine® factors commonly seen in overweight clients. More on my site. Note that this is not necessarily *the* way to go with any client, it is simply one way. You will notice also that Kathryn already has an astute awareness of her associations tied in with food. Note also my awareness of the likely association between my client being closer to her ideal weight and the sexual assault she suffered. With further EFT sessions, this is definitely an angle I would be exploring.

I lay out for you here an open window on my therapy room; the detective process as well as the reframes in action, for your learning. Along with me, you will be navigating the client's issues and rooting out the worthwhile avenues to go down (Gary's garbage and the gold), and naturally we will take some wrong turns along the way. I leave these in, in order to enhance your learning further.

You will also see here elegant examples of preframing; and explicitly marking out progress made with the client, to get round the apex effect. During the session, we move through the process of applying EFT to one specific movie, through the client's meta-feelings *about* letting it go, and on to bigger picture issues.

Due to the flowing nature of such sessions, you will forgive any obvious grammar, punctuation errors and so on. Naturally print will never do 100% justice to some of the fluid elements of such situations, such as change of speed, inflection, and so on. And, like most sessions, not all of the loose ends are neatly tied up at the end; - Kathryn is aware of the additional work required to see real world results. But the journey is that much easier with EFT…

**Me** – Hi Kathryn, what are we talking about today? We talked on the phone about weight issues…

**Kathryn** - Yeah, I'm thinking that I'd rather be lighter, and that kinda if I'm lighter, I am comfortable, I'll get up in the morning and just pull clothes out of my wardrobe and put them on rather than worrying about it…That sort of stuff. I'm not looking to sort of morph into some sort of super model…

**Me** – Sure

**K** – You know, be more myself and I just can't seem to get by it. I don't know. I have a gym membership, I've got a dog to walk, I've got kids to play with. I know that I eat properly and I just er, I just seem. I know obviously but…

**Me** – OK, cool…so do you think that it's kinda like, how do you experience the whole eating thing? Is there an element of compulsion about it? Or is there anything of that nature?

**K** – Em. Possibly. I guess I really love to – I love cooking…and I love cooking for other people and a lot of that is trying to demonstrate your affection for people. You know.

**Me** – Right. OK

K – You know. Yeah. If there's kinda junk like biscuits or whatever I do have a bit of a tendency that if I have one, I have ten…before I met my husband, I just didn't have stuff like that in the house, you know, I just didn't have sweet stuff…

Me – OK, so it was kinda like a reward thing when you were younger as well

K – I think so yeah. And I guess it's kinda, it's almost like, you know, celebration, what you do if something makes you sad, you need cheering up.

Me – Right.

K – There's quite a lot of stuff tied into that I guess.

Me – Definitely. It's definitely not like a one session wonder, you know? Cos you're kinda looking to collapse whatever all those associations are around it. You're looking to collapse your cravings …OK, 2 questions here. Have you ever had - are you diabetic?

K – No.

**Me** – No. Do you have any pancreas issues?

**K** – No.

**Me** – No. OK. Any kidney issues?

**K** – No. Why do you ask that?

**Me** – Well this is kinda like just one approach, which goes on weight. It goes on two issues... depends on what's more useful. The kidney collecting tubules can, if we have an abandonment isolation existence conflict ... which is like I'm basically alone here. Being abandoned. Feeling lost, to the point where my existence and survival is called in to question... OK, and even as we talk, I can see some stuff coming up.

**K** – Yeah.

**Me** – If there's that kind of stuff going on then, what that basically does is the kidney collecting tubules seize up like that and the edema and the excess water that the kidney would be draining is left in the body...and people think 'I can't lose weight' when that's not the reality. The reality is that they've got an abandonment conflict that's causing the kidneys to seize up. The other angle is if you're prone to diabetic type symptoms, you've got, low blood sugar. So the pancreas is maintaining sugar at a low level, which maintains hunger at a high level artificially. And the conflict behind that is more kind of the Fear Disgust Conflict. It can be a Fear Disgust Conflict or a Resistance Reluctance Conflict. For example, a woman in the work place, she gets a new boss, and her boss is overtly gay and she finds it disgusting. That's her perception. She develops diabetes. So it's just an example.

**K** – OK.

**Me** –Any of those emotional feelings ring a bell for you?

**K** – Em, the first one you were talking about…I guess there's quite a bit there. I kinda always felt, from a very young age like I was, I had to be quite grown up and erm sort of manage by myself. Like, I can't ever remember sort of, you know…..

**Me** – Can you think of a time when maybe you were lost or something like that, or you got lost?

**K** – Well. Funny… only a couple of months ago, my mum told me … I used to think that I had a recurring dream that I was falling down stairs and I kept having this image of me being at the bottom of the stairs crying. And she said, when I was a, well, a toddler I guess; she said the next door neighbour said to my Mum and Dad, "Go out and I'll babysit for Kathryn". And my Mum and Dad came back and I was sitting at the bottom of the stairs by myself, crying. And the neighbour had obviously put me to bed and then gone back to her house. And well she told me that cos we were talking about just, she didn't really go out when my brother and I were small cos she felt she couldn't … you know..

**Me** – Because of that incident?

**K** – Uh huh

**Me** – Right. OK. She came back, found out what had happened…..

**K**- …and was obviously really upset, you know.

**Me** – When would you say, you know, as you see it, the weight issue began?

**K** – Erm, well, it's one of those funny things. I thought, as a teenager, that I was fat. And I really really wasn't. I just wasn't skinny. And like when I look at my – my daughter's 11 now- and when I look at her now, I think "God, I hope you don't feel like I did." Erm, so the time when I actually put on most weight was probably after Sarah was born. She's gonna be seven this year. I went back to work and I got pneumonia, erm, stopped work and they thought that I had asthma after that. I had trouble with breathing and things and they put me on steroids. I put weight on after that and I'd put it down to the steroids because I thought it was that, but looking at it, I'm not sure it necessarily was that. You know. I don't know.

**Me** – What was going on for you around that time?

**K** – I was absolutely distraught to be going back to work. I thought I was totally doing the wrong thing. I'd been made redundant when I was pregnant and put into a new job. I hated it. I was passed over for a promotion when I was pregnant and was absolutely grief stricken.

**Me** – OK, what I'm trying to do is weed out the ones that are relevant and the ones that aren't.

**K** – I kinda see that episode as quite different and since changing, since doing reflexology and working with people and looking more into the emotional side, I'm pretty convinced that was – I was literally grief stricken to be going back to work and my body went like 'flop – that'll stop you working'. You know.

**Me** – Totally, totally. Tell me about the times that you kinda connect with the sense of abandonment or isolation. Cos it comes from the sense of – it's like an animal thing. It's going back on the basis that, although we're living in this kind of highly evolved society, right, we've still got age-old programs. So it's kinda like as if we were worms in the desert in this evolutionary sense and we're in this abandoned isolated environment – like a camel. So what other kind of times would come up for you like that?

**K** – OK. Well my dad was an alcoholic so sometimes he was not present, and because my mum had started working, you know, there would be occasions where he'd be drunk. I mean he wasn't violent but he wasn't top notch. One Hogmanay, my mum hardly ever drank, but she drank. We were round a neighbour's and my cousin was staying with us and they came back from the neighbours and my dad collapsed on the floor, and then she was in bed being sick.

**Me** – So mum was in bed and dad was…

**K** - … and I went to get the neighbour and they didn't wake up. They were obviously out of it as well. So I was looking after my little brother and my cousin and they were both quite hysterical, and really really frightened.

**Me** – You can connect that sense of abandonment with that?

**K** – Uh huh.

**Me** – OK, that's what we're looking for. That's kinda like the line I think we could do. Definitely look at the first one when you're young – and we'll take what we can get from that. I know you won't have a full conscious record of that first one…

**K** – No I don't.

**Me** – And, so what age would you have been in that one there?

**K** – Six or seven.

**Me** – OK. So you've not done EFT before?

**K** – Three years ago, I had hypnosis and EFT for depression.

**Me** – OK. How did you find that?

**K** – Absolutely amazing. I just had one session and it kinda really helped me flip how I was looking at things.

**Me** – OK, so your depression would have been after, either like a sexual conflict or a loss of territory conflict. Does that make sense?

**K**: Yeah. I was raped.

**Me** – OK… well, we won't go into it today cos it's easy to open all these cans of worms and not have the time to resolve them all. So let's talk about – how old would you have been at the bottom of the stairs?

**K** – I think I would have been like 1 or 2. Quite titchy.

**Me** – OK. And what can you remember from it?

**K** – I just thought it was a dream. I just had this image. I remembered stairs. I've got quite vivid pictures of the house we lived in and I remember the stairs and they were quite steep. And in this what I thought was a dream, it was almost like I float down stairs. But then I'm sitting at the bottom and I'm just kinda crying. I don't even know if I'm that upset – it's just –I don't know – confused? But it doesn't feel like I kinda know why I'm upset. It's not like when you hurt yourself and you're crying.

**Me** – So there would have been an emotionally comfortable time, before this started. Emotionally you would have felt fine. And there would have been a time after that, that you felt fine, emotionally. Can you kinda get a sense of where those might be in your head?

**K** – Yeah.

**Me** – OK. So you know about the process of EFT – I give you a set up, you repeat the set up.

**K** – Yeah I think so.

**Me** – So what will we call this? Let's call this a movie, what would it be called? 'The Time When I Was Lost When I Was Three' or 'Lost Little Kathryn' or 'I Feel Lost'. Give it a nice little….

**K** – Er, 'The Time When I Was Left'.

**Me** – OK. So, (Client taps round points, repeating language, mirroring me) (KC) Even though, I remember the time when I was left…kinda. I was two. I don't have much recollection of being two…I was doing the best that I could… I felt a bit confused, And lost. (TH) Being two years old.

**Me** – We'll just do a few rounds of tapping just to get you used to it. Just follow me round OK. (Client taps round points, repeating language, mirroring me) (TH) I was two… (EB) I was doing the best I could, (SE) I was doing the best I could…(UN) I was two… (CH) I was doing the best that I could…(CB) I didn't have many resources at two…(UA) What two year old does? (WR) What two year old does? (EB) Feeling lost. (SE) Feeling lost. (UN) And confused. (CH) I don't know where I am…. (UA) I don't know where I am.

**Me** – I'll just bring you out for a minute. So as you're talking to me about that day, are you looking at that Kathryn in the picture or are you looking through your own eyes, looking at the bottom of the stairs?

**K** – Looking at it I think.

**Me**- Looking at Kathryn?

**K** – Yeah.

**Me** – So, (Client taps round points, repeating language, mirroring me) (KC) Even though Kathryn's over there….(TH) And she's lost…(EB) she feels lost... (SE) I'm gonna step back, (UE) and witness, what's going on…(UN) I'm just gonna sit over here (CH) …that lost Kathryn over there. (CB) That lost Kathryn over there… (UA) That lost Kathryn over there…

**Me** – Good, and breathe out, so, as you kinda think about being down there at the bottom of the stairs; what comes up for you emotionally? What comes up for you physically in your body? What's going on for you? If you were to step into that Kathryn and relive it, what's coming up for you?

**K** – Em. More like kinda disappointment. Kinda feel it like there in my solar plexus…

**Me** – Describe this for me, is this kind of a tingling feeling, or…

**K** – More like a lump.

**Me** – A lump. OK. So bigger or smaller than the size of a fist?

**K** – Same (laughs)

**Me** – And does it feel soft or hard?

**K** – Hard.

**Me** – And if it was a colour, what colour would it be?

**K** – Black.

**Me** – So it's black. And what shape is it?

**K** – Lumpy (sighs).

**Me** – OK – so, (Client taps round points, repeating language, mirroring me) (TH) This black lumpy feeling... (EB) disappointment.... (SE) this black lumpy feeling. (UE) Disappointment... (UN) And maybe a bit sad. (CH) And a bit sad... (CB) This black lumpy feeling... (UA) this black lumpy feeling... (WR) this black lumpy feeling...and breathe out...good.

**Me** – Give that a number for me, how intense does the black lumpy feeling feel now?

**K** – 6

**Me** - (Client taps round points, repeating language, mirroring me) (TH) This black lumpy feeling… (EB) As I'm at the bottom of the stairs… (SE) This black lumpy feeling… (UE) I can see the stairs now, (UN) I notice their colour. (CH) This black lumpy feeling… (CB) Disappointment, (UA) Sadness. (WR) And maybe a bit hurt…remaining black lumpy feeling…

**Me** – What does it feel like now? Has it changed? Quality? Intensity? Tell me what's going on.

**K** – It's moved down to my stomach.

**Me** – OK. So we're just gonna do a round of tapping. What I want you to do is, close your eyes and I'm going to go verbally guide you round the points. And what I want you to do is, go into that feeling, go all the way into that feeling. Focus, intensely. All your concentration. Focus on that feeling. When the feeling changes, just allow it to change and continue to tap on whatever it is, wherever it moves to, whatever it does, that's absolutely fine, just allow it to do that. Pull all of your focus onto that physical feeling. (Client taps round points, mirroring me) (TH) Top of the head, good. (EB) Eyebrow point. Just breathe out… (SE) Side of the eye…

(UE) Under the eye (CH) Chin. Good…breathing out… (CB) Collar bone, all your focus on that physical feeling. (UA) Under the arm. (WR) Wrist…just allow it to be whatever it's gonna be. (TH) Top of the head…good (EB) Focus intensely on that physical feeling. (SE) Side of the eye… good. (UE) OK, under the eye, OK just breathe out and relax. With your attention and focus on the physical feeling, just tell me what's going on.

**K** – My stomach.

**Me** – Stomach OK. Give me a number for the stomach.

**K** – 5.

**Me** – 5. OK. And what's happening with the solar plexus?

**K** – It's started to move.

**Me** – OK. So let's just focus on the tummy OK. So top of the head. (Client taps round points, repeating language, mirroring me) (TH) All the focus on the tummy. (EB) Eyebrow point… (SE) Side of the eye… (UE) Under the eye…. (UN) Under the nose... (CH) And the chin point….whatever it changes to, just follow it. (CB) Collarbone, (UA) Under the arm…good…Just breathe out for me. Just describe what's going on now. Describe what it's like. Has the shape gone small?

**K** – It's gone. I just feel a bit winded.

**Me** – I have that effect on people (laughs). So I want you to again, just go back to that moment at the bottom of the stairs and just tell me what you're aware of with your physical body, emotionally etc.

**K** – I'm not sure. I seem a little bit sad. I keep seeing my own daughter instead of me.

**Me** – OK. So you're still seeing someone in the picture? As you think about what you're seeing in that event now; were you seeing that same picture before – before we started working - or were you seeing a different picture?

**K** – Different.

**Me** – OK. We'll just go back to the picture we saw before. I'm very thorough. Just tell me if there's any physical, emotional charge on it coming up for you.

**K** – (pause) No.

**Me** – OK. As we're going through, I just like to remind people that... cos it's easy to go to a session, come to the end of a session and we're still tapping on like a seven or an eight. And then they think, 'well, we're not making any progress here'. So I'll just say that you'll notice ... cos it happens so naturally, we just do it naturally, as soon as one aspect is resolved something that feels more important takes its place. So let's just go back to what you're seeing, which is, your girl. Ok, so let's just tap on the top of the head. (Client taps round points, repeating language, mirroring me) (TH) Focus on whatever is coming up for you in the physical body. And we'll just have you – in the mind's eye – look at that as we tap round the points. (EB) Eyebrow, (SE) side of the eye, (UE) under the eye, (UN) Under the nose, (CH) chin (CB) Collarbone (UA) under the arm... (WR) wrist. Just breathe out. So as you look at that picture, tell me what's coming up. What aspects are coming up for you emotionally?

**K** – It's actually OK. I'm just seeing her when she was that age. So it doesn't feel negative.

**Me** – OK, cool, so tune in again then, to being at the bottom of the stairs and I want you to just be there now. So I want you to really be there. Really notice the colour of the stairs. Is this inside stairs or outside stairs?

**K** – Inside stairs.

**Me** – So notice the floor covering, notice how light or dark it is, notice the dimensions and the space between the floor and the ceiling, notice the colour of the wall coverings and feel the clothes on your body and just tell me what's going on for you as you do that.

**K** - It all feels quite dark.

**Me** – And if there was an emotion connected to that feeling, what would that emotion be?

**K** – Fear.

**Me** – Yes, OK, that's what I was picking up…OK. (Client taps round points, repeating language, mirroring me) (UE) Under the eye… Just focus on that feeling…OK I've got like an 8 or a 9 on my radar over here, how am I doing? (client flushing, breathing deeply, some distress) (CB) Collar bone. (UA) Under the arm. If there's some self-talk going on on the inside, with this physical feeling, what's the self-talk? (still tapping) (WR) wrist…

**K** – Em. It's hard to put into words. It's like…you have to look after yourself.

**Me** – Is it like, 'maybe they're not coming back,' or 'I don't know where they are?'

**K** – You can't rely on anybody.

**Me** – OK, (TH) Top of the head… I can't rely on anyone. (EB) I feel abandoned. (SE) And alone… (UE) And maybe a little bit rejected… I just kinda say these things…some of them will hit the target, some of them won't. (UN) Abandoned. (CH) Rejected. (CB) Abandoned and rejected… (UA)…as I'm here at the bottom of the stairs… (WR) I can't rely on anyone, (TH) Not me.

**Me** – OK, Karate chop, just with me OK, (Client taps round points, repeating language, mirroring me) (KC) Even though I'm feeling abandoned, at the bottom of these stairs, I feel like I can't trust anyone, or maybe I trusted someone…and they broke that, I accept me anyway…I choose to accept all of me anyway, as a person. I'm doing the best that I can. (still tapping) (KC) Cos the thing about this situation is…it might just be possible, that as a two year old, I am assuming that this situation, at this moment, is only about this moment (TH) and it has got nothing to do with (EB) any other moments that came before, (SE) cos whoever it is that's abandoned me, (UE) is out there somewhere (UN) They're doing the best that they can. (CB) They're doing the best that they can… (UA) I can safely assume, that their intentions, (WR) are loving.

**Me** – OK. What's going on physically now?

**K** – 5

**Me** – OK. What emotionally, is still there for you?

**K** – I don't know. It's really hard…

**Me** – Sure. OK. You can just be aware of the physical feeling. So, (Client taps round points, repeating language, mirroring me) (KC) Even though I've still got some feeling left, I choose to accept myself, regardless. Despite this situation. I accept myself. While this situation is going on. Cos I'm still OK. People get through this kind of thing. I am a person. I can get through this. They're all somewhere else doing their thing. They're doing what they think they need to do. They're doing what they think they need to do. They have their reasons. I hope no-one judges me. For the things that I do. Because I always have my reasons. Right, wrong or otherwise. Their intentions were loving, and I can safely assume. That they didn't get up that morning, saying to themselves, 'Hey, how can I abandon Kathryn today?' …they were doing the best that they could – truly. Given their resources. And limitations. And the past experiences. That they've had. They're doing the best that they can. To give me love. And I can't blame them for that.. OK. Just tune back into what was going on for you. (TH) Top of the head… (EB) Eyebrow point, remaining feeling… (SE) remaining feeling… (UE) remaining feeling… (UN) under the nose… (WR) Wrist…and breathe out… Have some water (pause). Put yourself back at the bottom of the stairs again. Give me a number or just tell me what's going on. (client gestures to solar plexus region) What's going on in the solar plexus?

**K** – I'm aware of it but it's not an object.

**Me** – OK. So there's a feeling there. Give me a number for the feeling.

**K** – One.

**Me** – OK. Close your eyes. I want you to hold the want. I want you to go to that feeling and hold the want. Be in a state of want. Want and desire and intention. That that feeling begins to soften. Go to the feeling. Go into a place of having that feeling soften. Just have it soften. And as it softens, it will begin to flow. Just allow it to flow. (client breathes out) Softer still. Softer. Even softer. Softer. (synchronising "soften" instructions with client's out-breaths)…softer still. So with your focus and attention on the physical feeling, just tell me what's happening. Is it easier now? Good. So, go back to the bottom of the stairs. And just go into that and see it through your own eyes and just tell me anything that comes up. Anything, no matter if it's a quarter, or a half of a quarter, I want to know about it.

**K** – (pause) No it's OK. It's just like I'm looking at a picture.

**Me** – So you're still seeing Kathryn in the picture?

**K** – Yes.

**Me** – OK. So close your eyes and see that Kathryn in the picture and notice the angle that you see her from, and in your mind's eye, take a few steps closer towards that Kathryn. And tell me if anything comes up for you – emotional intensity….I'm picking up maybe a 4 anxiety, how am I doing?

**K** – A bit – in my head.

**Me** – And what does it feel like in your head? Does it feel like ….?

**K** – That feeling of when you get frightened, rather than when you're frightened of something.

**Me** – (Client taps round points, repeating language, mirroring me) (UE) under the eye…and (CB) collarbone…And just breathe out. See you notice that as we go a bit further in, we get more detail and more layers…we just peel the onion, you know? Here's what we do. Two fingers, both hands, on the eyebrow point. And I want you to see that same picture again, where Kathryn is quite close to you. You can do this with your eyes closed or your eyes shut. I want you to see that Kathryn and I want you to go like this (I demonstrate sudden and large breath out). As you see that Kathryn close to you, just a really big breath out. See that Kathryn and just a nice big breath out. Continue to see that Kathryn and just start tapping for me. (CB) Collar bone. (UA) Under the arm. (WR) Wrist. (UE) Under the eye. And breathe out, good. (pause) And tell me what's going on?

**K** – Nothing really there. Just like a picture I guess.

**Me** – So, go back to that picture and take a few steps closer towards that Kathryn so that you're almost face to face with her and you can really kinda feel her energy. And just tell me what's going on.

**K** – Em, I feel sick.

**Me** – OK. Just tap on the wrist. Just hold that picture. Tap on the wrist (WR) Breathe out. Don't worry I have that effect on people as well. I really need to work on it you know. (laughs) So here's what I want you to do. I want you to tap on Karate Chop point for me quite gently. Either that, or you can just hold it., whatever is more comfortable. I want you to see that Kathryn and I want you to have a conversation with her. Before we do that, I want you to imagine going to the morning that this event happened and imagine that you can see ahead and you know what's going to happen today. What is it that you would have needed to have known, at that point in time, to make it OK, that later today you were going to feel that way?

**K** – That mum and dad would come back. That it wasn't them that left you.

**Me** – And do they come back?

**K** – Yeah.

**Me** – Absolutely. Cos that's what Mums and Dads do. So have a conversation with that young Kathryn then and first of all, I want you to speak to her. And you can just ask her what she thinks she needs in this situation. It may be a hug, it may be support. Because the you that sits here with me now, knows more about this situation and has a different perspective on this. And you can offer her that support that she didn't have then. Whatever it is that she needs, just go ahead and give it to her. Take all the time you need. (pause)

OK, just continue to have that connection with her. And just let her know that Mum and Dad's intentions are good. And that if they had known that this was going to happen, they would have never allowed this to happen. They didn't know. And let that Kathryn then know that she's lovable, despite this event. Give her a hug. Let her know that whatever is going on here, it's going on because other people are operating out of their limitations. They are operating out of their limitations and they're doing the best they can with what they have available. This situation is just temporary, and that Mum and Dad are coming back.

OK, is there anything else that young Kathryn needs to know in order to make it OK that this is going to happen?

**K** – (breathing deeply, relaxed) No

**Me** - She's OK? OK. So go ahead and relive that event now in such a way that you're constantly reminding yourself, as you go through the event, of what you need to know, to make it OK.

**K** – OK (pause)

**Me** - Good. Any intensity? Anything there in that event at all?

**K** – No

**Me** – OK, I'm very thorough. I want you to go back to the start of that movie and run through it again from the start to the finish in your mind. And be quite intense about it. Try to get some intensity there because that is our opportunity to work on it, and then if anything comes up, just immediately stop, come out and let me know.

**K** – (pause) I feel a bit sad that she had to know that so young.

**Me** – At what point in the movie is this?

**K** – I don't know. It's hard to explain. When I was telling her what to do and that it would be OK, I felt such sadness that

**Me** – So this is your sadness of you now, about that Kathryn then, rather than...

**K** – Yes, OK.

**Me** –So let's just go over that. Where is it physically?

**K** – My eyes.

**Me** – Your eyes. So top of the head (Client taps round points, repeating language, mirroring me) (TH) this eye feeling, (EB) This feeling in my eyes. (SE) this sadness in my eyes... (client's intensity is obvious) so, I want you to see that moment again for me, see that Kathryn. And as you see that Kathryn, I want you to place your attention on your pinky finger. Just become aware of your little finger just feel what it feels like. And shift your attention to the physical heart, become aware of your physical heart and how it feels in your chest. Just begin to breathe through your physical heart, and just feel the air in and out of your heart, and see that Kathryn, as you breathe through your physical heart. And you can have the young Kathryn remind the older Kathryn that she did survive. Just feel the air in and out your physical heart. And that it's OK to have gone through something like that. As people experience circumstances; circumstances don't make a person. Circumstances reveal a person. Just breathe through the heart. OK, any intensity as you look at that?

**K** – Yeah, kinda feeling stupidity. I know these things that you said; it's true…it's kinda …

**Me** – There's a big 'but' there. What's the 'but'?

**K** – I feel annoyed with myself for letting these things affect me. I didn't even know what that was before.

**Me** – I've got that on the list and what we can do is go back to young Kathryn, and I want you to experience it through her eyes from start to finish. I really want you to experience it. If it's an eighth, or a quarter of a quarter of an eighth, I want to know about it, OK?

**K** – (pause) It's OK.

**Me** – It's like, a zero?

**K** – Yes.

**Me** – OK, just checking. So there's somewhat of a sense of 'I'm frustrated or angry at myself because I've allowed…' Help me out here. Is it like 'I've allowed that experience to…what?

**K** – Allowed ANY experience to stay with me, when I know logically, I know it's OK. I can say that whatever has gone before, has gone and it doesn't matter.

**Me** – So do you experience that as 'I'm angry at myself' or 'I'm angry at the world' or…

**K** – Myself.

**Me** – Myself. OK. Is it like frustration or…

**K** – I think actual anger.

**Me** – Where is it in your physical body?

**K** – Heart.

**Me** – Heart. OK so, (Client taps round points, repeating language, mirroring me) (KC) Even though, I've had some experiences, and I'm the only person, to have had certain experiences, nobody else in the world has had these experiences, and I've managed to hold on to them, somehow. I can accept myself anyway….or at least Stewart wants me to….good luck with that... (laughs) (Client taps round points, repeating language, mirroring me) (TH) I'm angry at myself... (EB) I'm angry at me. (SE) I'm angry at me. (UE) Course it's all about me (laughs)... (UN) I've allowed myself to hold on to these things...(CH) Logically, I know better, (CB) Emotionally, it's a different story, (UA) Of course, I would never point the finger at anyone else for this... (WR) And self-blame is no better....true statement?


**K** – Yeah.


**Me** – (TH) Because the rest of me, (EB) Is beginning to wonder, (SE) If this self-blame, (UE) is actually achieving anything at all. (UN) It's maybe not that useful. (CH) Maybe what I need to do is... (CB) offer myself... (UA) some acceptance, (WR) some self acceptance. (TH) I need to allow myself. (EB) that space... (SE) and love... (UE) Cos we go through life, (UN) trying to get love, (CH) from Mum, (CB) from Dad. (UA) from anybody else... (WR) maybe I need to love me first. (TH) I choose to accept all of me. (EB) Without judgement (SE) I'm a person like any other, (UE) I've got the same deservingness, (UN) of love, (CH) and everything else, (CB) as the baby born next to me in the hospital, (UA) and this self-blame doesn't get me anywhere. (TH) Top of the head. Part of me wants to hold on to it. (EB) The rest of me knows better. (SE) It's keeping me safe. (UE) That's the most ridiculous thing I've ever heard (UN) I choose to move on, (CH) I can accept me anyway, (CB) without judgement... (UA) I would never judge anyone else that way... (WR) But I'm trying to judge me like that. (TH) Others' judgements of me.... (EB) Reflect their limitations. OK, finish off round the points... (SE) (UE) (UN) (CH) (CB) (UA) (WR)

Good. Breathe out. So give me a number about that aspect of holding on to it.

**K** – 3.

**Me** – Find the 3 in your physical body for me. OK. Are you getting anything in your physical body? OK. (client looks visibly distressed, breathing deeply, flushed face) (EB) Eyebrow point. (WR) And wrist. I've got like a 9 or a 10 sadness on my radar here, how am I doing? What was coming up for you? Have you got a picture or a memory or something? (UE) Under the eye…

**K** – I think I just em…I don't really know.

**Me** – OK, so I'm just going to tap on your hand here with your permission. OK? You just focus on your physical heart for me OK? Let me take all the weight of the arm, and just relax. Breathing through the physical heart. Feel the air going through. (pause) What was the memory? What was coming up for you there?

**K** – I'm thinking about my Nana.

**Me** – Nana. OK. Tell me about Nana.

**K** – She's in a nursing home. She isn't very well. My grandad died twenty years ago. She's been living alone since then.

**Me** – Is your sadness about her aloneness or…

**K** – Yeah. It's quite painful thinking about that. It probably comes over selfish. I think, 'I wouldn't like to be like that'. I think that's probably why it's so painful. I don't know why that popped into my head.

**Me** – OK. What's going on for you now intensity-wise?

**K** – Better

**Me** – (client visibly improved) OK, so I just want to double-check what we've done so far, so… First of all, go back to whatever you've got. Whatever intensity, whatever feelings are there about holding on to issues of the past and just let me know intuitively (snaps fingers) if there's anything coming up.

**K** – Nothing.

**Me** – Nothing. Nothing at all?

**K** - What comes into my head when you say that is that I think it will come back. It's like I believe it and I don't believe it.

**Me** – OK. So what we're talking about is, any feelings about having held on to that. OK. So we've got the Nana memory written there up on the board and we'll come back to that. So let's go back to the fear that this is going to come back. Tell me about worrying about that and how you experience that.

**K** – I just want to be totally free from past actions and feelings and things that have happened. And in equal measure, I believe that that is possible and also impossible.

**Me** – OK. So just to point out; we've shifted aspects. We've done the groundwork and now we've jumped to meta-feelings about this experience and then meta-feelings about all experience. We'll work directly on this up here. Obviously, from a therapeutic point of view, we want to be collapsing all the issues that are down here, as we all do. We'll work a little bit of time on this and then, if we've got anything left, we'll maybe work on the Nana picture.

**K** – If there's an emotional aspect of it, I guess it's that there's a fear that I won't be free from it.

**Me** – So there's a part of you that feels like you're holding on to certain things.

**K** – I don't even know what they are though.

**Me** – Right. It's the kind of awareness that, 'I'm holding onto things for a reason. I don't know why that is, but bla bla bla'. OK. We've all got issues but we kinda go through these experiences and from the point of view of our unconscious mind, if we're very young – like under six years old – it's a survival issue. All our unconscious mind is interested in is getting through this event and surviving. The unconscious mind isn't really interested in – if we hold on to an aspect of this issue, it may turn into obsessive behaviour in the future. It may turn into addictions that are not particularly useful. But the point being that, whenever we went through those experiences initially, there was a purpose to be holding on to that. At that time, it was either for survival, protection or safety. So you can get a sense of safety from the fact that, whatever your unconscious mind thinks, perceives is there – it had a good reason at that time. It's just not that useful anymore. So, (Client taps round points, repeating language, mirroring me) (KC) Even though, I don't feel safe…or comfortable…I may feel unprotected, I'll let these things go, I'll let all these things go, part of me is telling me that I'm not going to feel safe, I'm not safe, I don't feel safe, I want to let this go, but I don't feel safe, I'm conflicted, but I want to let this stuff go, part of me does want to let go, but I don't feel safe, so all those experiences from the past, I learned from, I went through them, and I survived, I learned enough, to still be here, and that's enough right now…(TH) I want to hold on to these events…(EB) I want to let them go…(SE) I want to hold on, (UE) I want to let them go…(UN) Let me be free…(CH) I want to hold on to them… (CB) I'm not safe…(UA) I don't feel safe anyway (WR) Safety is an illusion…(TH) That we tell ourselves, (EB) Just like comfort and anything else…(SE) Cos anyone who's ever been through anything…(UE) Will tell you…(UN) That it can all be taken away, (CH) Very quickly…(CB) We like to pretend that we're safe…(UA) We like to tell ourselves that we're comfortable (WR) Just so as we feel OK….(TH) And that's fine (EB) Letting go of these issues…(SE) Letting it all go…(UE) I accept myself anyway, (UN) With it, (CH) (CB) (UA) (WR) Letting these issues go…

**Me** – As we talk about what we were talking about, what's coming up in your body, physically? What do you feel? Be aware of the sensations.

**K** – There's a kind of slightly winded feeling.

**Me** – So close your eyes and go there. Go to that feeling. And talk to that feeling on the inside and to let it know all the experiences of the past were useful for the purpose of getting you here at this point. And that's OK. And I want you to accept with open arms this feeling, because we go through life pushing away these parts of us that we don't like, and rejecting them and they come back and we push them away and they come back. And I just want you to accept it with open arms. And know, in a pure sense in yourself, that this part has nothing but the best intentions for you. It has nothing but your safety, your comfort, and protection at heart. It's only intention is nothing but good for you and I just want you to acknowledge that. Accept it and thank it. Thank it for looking after you. Tell it that you accept it without reservation. And I want you to allow it to soften. Just allow it to be. Soften and flow...I want you to imagine that the top of your head opens up and a solvent liquid of some kind comes down through your head down to that part. It might be water, it might be lovely rose quartz water – gallons and gallons of it, more than enough, all the way down and just massaging that feeling. Just softening the feeling even more. It softens even more. Softer still. Even softer. With your attention on the physical feeling, just tell me what's happening please.

**K** – (Coughing) I think it's gone.

**Me** – Let it soften even more. Softer still (pause). Softer still. What's happening now?

**K** – (Coughing).

**Me** – I think we may be tapping into whatever it is around the asthma emotionally. So what are you aware of?

**K** – I feel quite "level".

**Me** – Is that a good kind of level...or a ….

**K** – A good kind of level (laughs).

**Me** – So what are your thoughts about feeling safe, letting things go?

**K** – That yes it's the right thing to do isn't it?

**Me** – OK…that's the correct answer I have on my card here…(laughs)…I'm detecting hesitation.

**K** – I'm finding it quite hard to articulate what I'm feeling.

**Me** – Are you feeling any resistance, intuitively?

**K** – I still get that slight irritation almost. OK, there's a little bit of me that thinks it's a little bit wrong to be so self-reflecting.

**Me** – OK. Is that like 'I don't deserve to spend time with me.' Or is it like….

**K** – Yeah. I think so. I just…

**Me** – So what would happen if you were really self-reflective?

**K** – I just wouldn't move forward.

**Me** – What kind of person would you be if you were self-reflective? Would you be OK?

**K** – Selfish.

**Me** – Would you be a likable... like, people don't like me.

**K** – Yeah.

**Me** – And what else could happen? What other down sides could there be to being self-reflective?

**K** – I wouldn't be able to help other people.

**Me** – Why is that?

**K** – I don't know, I just blurted that out.

**Me** – OK, so, (Client taps round points, repeating language, mirroring me) (KC) Even though, I might not deserve…to spend time on me, I can spend time on others, and definitely spend time on the kids, and everyone else…but I'm last on that list…I don't deserve it.

**Me** – Where is it in your physical body, that feeling?

**K** – My throat.

**Me** – (Client taps round points, repeating language, mirroring me) (TH) I don't deserve.

**Me** – Anything coming up for you now? I can see something there…

**K** – I just keep thinking of one of my friends. She kind of takes up the whole room and she spends the whole time talking about herself….Cycling round all her problems and not changing anything.

**Me** – That's not annoying at all is it? (laughs). So, (Client taps round points, repeating language, mirroring me) (KC) Even though I'm scared…to spend time with me, because of what other people might think…I'm focussed externally…I'm focussed on others, and their judgements of me? (raised eyebrows)

**K** – No…I'm not sure…

**Me** – OK, so fill in the blank for me – "If I'm too self-reflecting, then "blank""?

**K** – Then my life will be empty because I won't pay attention to others?

**Me** – OK. Right here, (Client taps round points, repeating language, mirroring me) (KC) Even though, I've built up all these good reasons, not to pay attention to me…to feel less than worthy, I choose to feel worthy anyway. I choose to be free.

**Me** – There's a couple of directions we could go. Which aspect feels strongest to you? Is it 'others might judge me' or 'I'm not worthy of it' or some other angle?

**K** – OK. I do believe to an extent that it doesn't really matter what other people think of me. People that I love, that's different. I want to be a good person. It's complicated isn't it? Maybe it's to protect myself and I do care what other people think.

**Me** – We go through life and we have experiences and we make generalisations. The trouble is, when we pick up a belief from something we've perceived in the outside world…once we've picked it up, it becomes active upon us as well as our judgement of the outside world. What I'm getting is, whatever charge emotionally, is there for you, around experiences where other people have been taking up too much of the lime light, you – if your judgements, beliefs of them weren't there about them being them then you would feel free-er to allow yourself to be you. And it's maybe those beliefs that are hindering your ability to let your own stuff go. Does that make sense?

**K** – Yes. Uh huh.

**Me** – Well, generally here, we looked at the early experience of that incident on the stairs, and we resolved that. And what we got out of that was kinda like a meta-judgement about it. And we have that here as a pattern going on..."OK I feel like this but, it's really bad to feel like that." I think there's definitely an element of "it's not safe to be myself or do whatever it is that I want to do, because if I am like that, I know I won't be a good person. I'll not be a meaningful person.' So I think we'll do some general tapping around it, with the proviso that as we do it, we know that we're not going to collapse mountains here, we'll do what we can with the time we have left. I'll just have a ramble. Just go with it OK? (laughs)... (Client taps round points, repeating language, mirroring me) (KC) Even though... I'm imposing all these limitations on me... I'm doing the best that I can, even here and now. And then when I had all those experiences...all those stories that I told myself ...fairytales and legends, that stuff mattered...and that what people think of me matters, And about all this persona that I've got to maintain, The trouble is, it's exhausting me...because being me, and being true to myself, is effortless, that's who I really am, and that doesn't consume energy, and I don't need any extra food to do that, I just be me... And the me is fine. And the me is worthy. And the me is lovable. And I've convinced myself somehow. Along the journey, by way of all these experiences. Which happened TO me, and are not my responsibility. That somehow it's different, and that somehow those things mattered, when the rest of me knows better, and I choose to accept myself without judgement.(pause)

**Me** - ... Cos I think what we're getting down to, is a core of self-acceptance. (Client taps round points, repeating language, mirroring me) (KC) Even though...when others judge me, they're only reflecting back, the limitations, they place on themselves, true statement?

**K** – I guess. Yeah.

**Me** – If I judge you, for doing something...that's how I limit myself, isn't it? "Kathryn's done that, she's..... you know I would never do that..." In other words, if I did that, I would be unacceptable. I would be void of meaning (laughs) if I did that. Who does she think she is? It's like the box we keep ourselves in isn't it, because even when you're walking down the street, we intuitively judge people, you know. We have to. We do it intuitively from the experiences that we've had, from the generalisations that we've made. The point is, we have to do it, because if we didn't have these beliefs that function so automatically, then we couldn't get through life. If I had to learn that this table is solid and that's a door and so on every day, we'd never be able to function.

**K** – Sometimes our judgements are right, as well though. The feelings you have.

**Me** – Well, a better way to think of it, is whether they're useful or not. So, who's this friend that's kind of loud mouth and stuff? Or you can give her a name.

**K** – June.

**Me** – So June is – she does what she does. But it's fair to say that June probably has issues; and in doing what June does, she's probably trying to get attention, to get love. Her unconscious mind is taking this opportunity to vent the stuff that's in there. She's looking to get love and that's all we do. And when we're younger, we have Mum and Dad and we learn 'Oh, if I behave like this, I get more kisses and cuddles.' So we spend the rest of our lives trying to get love in whatever way we can. And this is the only means, within her life experiences and limitations and beliefs, that June has to do that. It's kinda like a bully. They've arrived at this place where they've got no other means to get attention. If they had any other way to do it, they would.

**K** – It's sad.

**Me** – It is sad. Because we've got limited resources. We get limited attention. We get limited love. And again, Mums and Dads are doing their best. What they can. And that's what we do. So, generally, go easy on yourself, in terms of self judgement and things like that. Go easy on yourself in terms of whatever kind of situations your dealt with. And a way to do that is to begin to wonder what could be behind this situation that is annoying me or that I'm judging. If we saw the bigger picture ….we just assume …. because we're in that moment of trauma or anxiety or whatever it is, and we just assume at that moment in time that that's what it is and that that's what the moment is all about. 9 times out 10, people have some pretty big stuff that got them to that place. So, I think we'll leave it here for today…cos we're over time and we've covered that initial event quite nicely and hopefully you get a sense of being able to think in terms of the bigger picture. If we were doing further session would you be sticking with the weight issue?

**K** – Yeah

**Me** – OK, well, we can hold ourselves in a place of unhealing for a zillion reasons. But they're all to do with the emotional attachment behind those specific events. I would be more inclined to go back to individual, specific events. OK, so, hopefully my ramblings have been useful. Has that been useful today?

**K** – Definitely,

**Me** – OK, thank you for coming in.

**K** – Thank you.

# ~ 12 ~

# Live Transcript Of An EFT Reframing Session: Gillian - Anxiety

I had a single session with Gillian (name changed) – a warm, sensitive, and caring woman, looking for emotional relief from anxiety and panic symptoms.

Listen in as we track back through relevant memories and work on an early experience, making substantial progress along the way.

I had chatted briefly on the phone beforehand with Gillian. As you know, there is some small talk and bridge-building work to be done with clients who are completely new to the process and this does make up some of the dialogue, but I leave it in for continuity.

You will witness many techniques in action here, including straight EFT, reframing, colour of pain; and some techniques to keep the client out of fight/flight, including physical-isation of emotional issues, and shifting between past and present tense language. Also, you will notice me using some unorthodox tapping routines around different points, missing out the setup, tapping round body points during the setup, and so on, as I intuit what I believe the client needs in that moment.

And, with the written transcript of the session, we can readily pick out where the client shifts emotional aspects through the ELT, from anger to sadness, sadness to fear, and so on.

Here's how it went.

**Me -** Hi Gillian, thanks for coming in today, so what are we working on…you mentioned agoraphobia.

**Gillian -** Well yeah, I suppose I had agoraphobia for quite a long time.

**Me -** Right.

**G -** And panic attacks, I'm unable to use public transport I have to go everywhere by car, which is my car. You know?

**Me -** Sure…tell me a bit more.

**G -** I don't know . . . it's maybe about . . . maybe two, three years that the kinda anxiety and panic attacks and everything were really bad and there was probably for about a year where I was unable to leave the house at all even going into the garden, I just couldn't do. It has improved a lot; once I started getting a bit better and I learned how to drive that just kinda changed my life and I starting going out a lot more, I had a lot more freedom. I guess I just feel stuck in a rut at the moment because all the feelings are still there. Like I could probably go on the train right now and be fine but . . . it's anything where I feel I don't have any control of the situation. Like I said I could probably get a train every day for a month and be fine, but there is always that thing in the back of my mind, that I'm like, what if I start to panic. What would I do?

**Me -** OK.  If we were to go down to the station just now and get on a train, what would be the worse aspect of it?  Would it be there are a lot of people here or I don't have a lot of space or...

**G -** None of that at all.  My worry would just be "what if I start to panic".

**Me -** What if I start to panic.  OK.  So it's kinda like you would panic and then have a panic attack.

**G -** Yeah.

**Me -** Right, OK.  So, can you remember the first time you had a panic attack? . . . Is it something you've had for a long time?

**G -** Yeah, I had kinda serious anxiety problems when I was about seven.  I've seen numerous psychologists and psychiatrists, had numerous drugs flung at me.

**Me -** Are you taking any meds at the moment?

**G -** Yes, I'm actually on medication at the moment.

**Me** - Tell me about that?

**G** - Venlafaxine.

**Me** - Venlafaxine, OK.

**G** - I started when I was 19.

**Me** - What is the translation of that, Venlafaxine is that basically just a . . .

**G** - It's an anti-depressant; I think it is quite well, kinda, known for treatment of anxiety and depression but anxiety . . .

**Me** - Like generalised anxiety. OK, so you've had like these anxiety type symptoms since you were seven?

**G** - Yeah.

**Me** - OK, so what was going on around then?

**G** - Umm, my Mum and Dad split up, and I started just . . . it was anytime I was away from my Mum I got really, really anxious. I was convinced that she was going to die, that something was going to happen to her. So I just felt I always had to be there to make sure she was OK. I used to sit up throughout the night to make sure that she was OK. I mean she was fine, there was nothing wrong with her, apart from the fact that her marriage had just broken up and she was now struggling with being a single parent with me and my brother. I was just so terrified that something was going to happen to her.

**Me** - OK, I can see there are emotions going on just now, is that fair to say? As you were talking about that just there?

**G** - Yeah.

**Me** - So you know about the SUDS scale we use, yeah? Describe how that emotion feels in your body.

**G** - Just a strange feeling kinda from here down to here.

**Me** - So, midriff, OK.

**G** - Yeah.

**Me** - Yeah, OK. And I had that at kinda 6, 7, on my radar over here, how am I doing? Yeah. OK. Well it's a good place to start to get you used to the tapping and stuff as well and to see the points. So you're on these meds just now?

**G -** Yeah.

**Me -** So I'll get you tapping on you, I won't tap on you unless you're comfortable to do that. So we'll start out, so just mirror me, just tap where I tap. So, tune back into your physical body, to the feeling you were talking about as you were kind of watching over your Mum and making sure that she was OK. Can you get any of that going on just now?

**G -** Yeah.

**Me -** OK, (Client taps round points, repeating language, mirroring me) (UE) under the eye, a bit of colour change there. Is it the same kinda feeling?

**G -** Yeah.

**Me -** OK, so just mirror me tapping round and what I want you to do is just focus intensely, all your internal focus is on the physical feeling, on the physical feeling, not in the head, on the physical feeling. OK and tap here for me, good, good, it's a kinda multitasking thing. Good, under the eye.

So what's the best way to describe this feeling?  Is it anxiety or are you worried or scared?

**G -** Probably all of them.

**Me -** OK, so just take a breath, take a breath out.  OK, so what picture have you got going on there?  Like in your mind's eye, as you think about Mum and you look over, are you seeing her in bed or whatever?  Tell me what's going on there.

**G -** Yes, I mean I was just thinking about her in bed and being asleep . . . and just kinda watching over her.

**Me -** Right, in case…?

**G -** In case . . . I don't know . . . in case something happened to her . . . just watching her to make sure she was OK.

**Me -** So, we'll get you kinda repeating what I'm going to say.  I'll just have a ramble.  I appreciate this is totally new and weird stuff so we'll just go with it.  So (Client taps round points, repeating language, mirroring me) (KC) Even though I've got to watch over Mum…. 'cause I don't know what is going to happen, and I've got this fear in my body… I accept myself anyway. OK, how did that kinda sit with you; - the notion of "I accept myself?" Does it . . .

**G -** No. (Laughing).

**Me -** Yeah, 'cause some folks are kinda like "no". OK, (Client taps round points, repeating language, mirroring me) (KC) I want to accept myself anyway, despite the fact that I've got these feelings...(TH) these feelings. This fear, just repeat this with me. This fear, (EB) this fear, (SE) this fear... (UE) this fear, (UN) this fear in my body (CH) this fear in my body...(CB) this fear in my body, (UA) this fear in my body...good and (WR) this fear in my body. OK, and breathe out. So the reason we're saying these statements, the only reason we are saying these statements is the intention is to keep you focused on the feeling as we are tapping round. The idea is we bring these feelings up and we tap them down, that's what we are doing basically. So tell me what is going on in the midriff, any relief or not relief?

**G -** Umm, I feel a bit kinda calmer.

**Me -** Calmer OK. Give me a number if you could, I keep going back to these numbers because it's the best way of measuring it, you know what I mean? So what number do you have for that feeling now?

**G -** Umm, maybe about 3 or 4, and it started out about 7 or 8.

**Me -** OK, so tap here for me. (Client taps round points, repeating language, mirroring me) (KC) So, even though I've got some remaining fear…and a part of me thinks it is a good idea to hold on to this… because it might be protecting me some how, I accept myself anyway, or at least I want to…and I choose to respect who I am anyway. (TH) I choose to respect who I am anyway… (EB) I choose to respect who I am anyway, (SE) focus intensely on that physical feeling, (UE) (UN) (CH) that's all the focus. (CB) OK. . . collar bone. . . total focus on the physical feeling. . . (UA) OK under the arm . . . and breathe out. . .OK . . . (KC) Even though I've got some remaining feelings... (TH) about this scene with Mum, (EB) I deeply and completely…. (SE) love and accept myself anyway… (UE) or at least Stewart wants me to (Laughing)… (UN) good luck with that. (Laughing) OK. (CB) collar bone . . . (UE) under the eye. OK, give me a number for what is going on just now?

**G -** Maybe a 2, 3.

**Me -** 2 or 3. So you can close your eyes if it helps you focus better but I just want you to focus on the physical feeling, and just kinda describe it for me, is it bigger or smaller than the size of a fist?

**G -** Bigger.

**Me -** Bigger. Is it hot or cold?

**G** - Cold.

**Me** - Cold, OK. What colour is it, if it had a colour what would it be?

**G** - Green.

**Me** - Green, OK. And what shape is it?

**G** - Circular.

**Me** - Circular. So a green, cold circle, that's bigger than the size of a fist. Does it move around, does it go up or down or anywhere?

**G** - No.

**Me** - OK, so, (Client taps round points, repeating language, mirroring me) (TH) this green cold circle, (EB) green cold circle … (SE) (UE) (UN) green cold circle, that's big in size… (CH) (CB) (UA) green cold circle…Has it changed quality in anyway, like more dispersed or less dispersed or . . . ?

**G** - It doesn't seem so intense.

**Me -** Doesn't seem so intense. So, just for a minute, just focus on the feeling and using the feeling as your guide, I just want you to track back in time. So just focusing on the feeling, remember a time, early in life when you felt this same kind of feeling, just allow a picture to come up and meet you. Just focus on the feeling. And just tell me when you've got a picture.

**G -** (pause) OK.

**Me -** OK, you've got a picture yeah. You don't have to tell me what it is and what you are doing, but if you are comfortable doing so then go ahead, or if you'd rather keep it to yourself . . .

**G -** My Mum taking me and my brother to meet my Dad because we were supposed to be going to stay with my Dad for the weekend and I didn't want to go, but he dragged me away it was really upsetting, my Mum was crying and I was crying . . .

**Me -** Right, OK. So at this time as you are there now in that moment in time now, does that feeling that you've got feel like "this is a familiar feeling" or does it feel like "this is new I've not had this before?"

**G -** It feels familiar.

**Me -** It feels familiar, OK. So focus again on the physical feeling and track back a bit further in time and just remember a time even earlier in life when you felt those same feelings...

**G -** (pause) OK.

**Me -** OK, so tell me what's going on in this one?

**G -** Umm, I'm at my Dad's house and, I don't know, it must be in the middle of the night and . . . I couldn't sleep and I went downstairs and . . . he was sleeping in the chair, and it was like a horror film or something on TV and I just remember sitting at the side of his chair . . . waiting for him to wake up.

**Me -** OK. So come on back out and we'll do a bit of tapping on that anyway. (Client taps round points, mirroring me) (EB) Eyebrow point. So, what's going on, I've got an 8 sadness, something like that?

**G -** Yeah.

**Me -** What's going on when you think about that then? OK, so let's kind of treat this as like a little kinda mini movie, this kinda going downstairs, seeing Dad and waiting for him and so on. So if this was like a movie how long would the movie be?  Would it be like a minute or two minutes or more or less or?

**G -** Umm, about an hour.

**Me -** So this is from before this happened and things felt emotionally comfortable at that point, yeah?  And then you went downstairs . . .give me like the gist of it . . . when you were downstairs was it fear about him not waking up or what's going to happen or sadness or what was going on?

**G -** Umm, sadness I just felt really alone, because I guess I kinda felt if he did wake up he wouldn't be much use anyway.

**Me -** OK. So this is about an hour this movie. So in this movie if there were a couple of emotional crescendos in the movie that we could work on, could you pick them out?

**G -** Yeah.

**Me -** Good.  So let's pick out whatever the first one is, and tell me a bit about what is going on there?

**G -** Umm, kinda getting downstairs and seeing him sitting in the chair and not knowing what to do and...

**Me -** …So where are you at this point? Are you on the stairs looking down or…?

**G -** Just standing at the living-room door.

**Me -** Cool. So keep that picture there. Are you right or left handed?

**G -** Right.

**Me -** Right handed. Keep that picture in your mind's eye as we tap through. So what's the first kind of emotion you are aware of, as you are standing outside the living-room door, tell me what the first thing you feel, or the first concern you've got, you know what I mean?

**G -** I guess, just not knowing what to do, whether to go in or to just stay there.

**Me -** OK, so with me… (Client taps round points, repeating language, mirroring me) (KC) Even though I don't know what to do…I'm not sure whether to go in or not… I'm only age, what age are you?

**G -** Umm, six.

**Me** - Six. I am only six…in this moment, I am doing the best I can, with the resources that I have, I'm six years old, I don't have many resources at six years old…who does? (TH) Top of the head. So what I want you to do now is, as we tap round these points just tune in. Really, really find the feeling in your physical body, of this "I don't know what to do." Focus is important. Do you feel it? Have you got it going on in your physical body? Yeah? OK. And it will change probably as we tap, and that is absolutely fine, whatever it changes to allow it to change, whatever it changes, if it moves around, changes quality that's absolutely fine, just tap on whatever we are doing. And I'm going to; we are going to just do some reminders as we go round. (TH) this feeling, (EB) I don't know what to do, (SE) this feeling, (UE) I don't know what to do… (UN) whether to go in, (CH) or not, (CB) this feeling… (UA) this feeling, (WR) tap on the wrist there. This feeling (TH) I don't know whether to go in… (EB) or not… (SE) side of the eye, (UE) I don't know if it's safe, (UN) this feeling… (CH) this feeling, (CB) focus on your physical body . . . (UE) under the eye . . . and breathe out for me. OK, good. So just consider that scene again, just standing outside the front of the living-room door and just tell me if things have changed what number have you got?

**G** - (pause) 2, 3

**Me** - 2, 3. And what is that 2, 3?

**G -** I still feel a little bit uncertain, but not being worried about it.

**Me -** A worried feeling, a kind of uncertainty but it has shifted aspects somehow in someway. So it's a kind of, tell me more about that, as you're standing outside the living-room door.

**G -** Umm, I guess being unsure but being OK with . . . being unsure.

**Me -** OK, cool. Where do you feel that in your body?

**G -** Across my shoulders.

**Me -** OK. Just tap on the collar bone for me please. And just be in that moment at that point in time. Just focus on that sense of unsure. (Client taps round points, repeating language, mirroring me) (CB) I'm unsure. (UE) I'm unsure. Good, OK and just follow me around the points, and say the words with me. (KC) Even though I've got some of this unsure feeling left...and part of me thinks it's a good idea to hold on to it, the rest of me knows better... this is one moment... in a six year old's life, in one life, in one house, in one street, on one planet, and I live beyond it... (TH) top of the head, remaining feelings...(EB) remaining feelings, (SE) remaining feelings...(UE) (UN) (CH) (CB) remaining feelings...and (UA) under the arm, and breathe out, good. Tell me what's happening physically and emotionally?

**G -** I feel really relaxed.

**Me -** Cool, that's good. What was happening with the specific feeling you had at that moment in time? Has it dispersed or?

**G -** Yeah.

**Me -** OK, like a zero or is it...

**G -** Yeah.

**Me -** Good, so let's just continue on with this movie where the next thing that happens is what...you go into the room? OK. So, what I like to do is look at that, moment by moment, moment by moment. As you are going into the room, see that in your mind's eye, OK.

**G -** OK.

**Me -** Just going into the room does that bring anything up for you?

**G -** Umm, I can feel a bit of fear.

**Me -** (Client taps round points, mirroring me) (CB) And tap here, OK, good. And just take your other hand and (UE) under the eye, and just kind of focus on that moment. Just that moment, don't run ahead in the movie, just that moment of going into the room. Just going into the room, just focus all your attention on that, OK. (UA) And under the arm. (WR) And just see the door opening and remember the colour of the door and be aware of the dimensions of the room and (TH) where the ceiling is and where the floor is and just walk into the room and . . . just walk into the room. (EB) Good, OK, eyebrow. Tell me what is going through your head as you walk into the room?

**G -** Umm . . . just what do I do . . . umm do I wake him up? Will he be mad if I wake him up?

**Me -** (TH) OK, top of the head. (Client taps round points, repeating language, mirroring me) What do I do... (EB) what do I do, (SE) what do I do now (UE) I am not sure what to do (UN) will I wake him up...(CH) or not... (CB) this unsure feeling...(UA) I accept my feelings anyway, (WR) this unsure feeling. Good, and breathe out for me. And focus on your physical feelings, take a second if you want and really find what's going on in your body. Really find it. (UE) Good, under the eye. This unsure feeling, (UN) under the nose... (CH) this unsure feeling (CB) Collar bone, I don't know what to do (UA) always focus on the physical body. I don't know what to do... (WR) at this point I don't know what to do, just breathe out, good. What's the number of the unsure feeling? How's that doing?

**G -** I feel a bit better.

**Me -** Better like a 1 or a 2 or a 5 or a . .

**G -** Umm a 4.

**Me -** 4, OK. Umm, let's just tap here. (TH) On top of the head, remaining unsure feeling (EB) I can feel it in my body, (SE) it's been living (UE) rent free (UN) in me (CH) for twenty years (CB) this remaining feeling (UA) I accept myself anyway (TH) remaining feeling (EB) I respect myself despite it, (SE) remaining feeling (UE) I'm OK with or without it (UN) I'm OK (CH) with or without it (CB) OK, as a person. (UA) this remaining feeling (TH) at this point I was six years old… (EB) I don't know what to do, (SE) good, relax. Tell me what's going on in terms of . . .in this moment in time?

**G -** Umm, just thinking that I want to be at home with my Mum, wondering if she was OK.

**Me -** Right.

**G -** What if she has had a fire, umm, there had been firemen at school that day and they had given us a talk on the dangers of house-fires and everything, and that was why I couldn't sleep, I was so terrified there was going to be a fire.


**Me -** OK. So between these two knuckles, and about an inch or two in, between the two tendons there, with two fingers, just tap on this one point continuously and we are just going to do some bizarre eye movements. I just want you to focus on that moment; on I'm unsure of what is going to happen here. I really want to be with Mum. Is Mum OK? All those self-talk things. OK. So we're tapping here, we are holding all those thoughts. And I'm going to instruct you to move your eyes around, while we do it. So, here's the thing and you can close your eyes if it's more comfortable. We are going to move the eyes, and imagine that your nose is the centre of a giant clock face and you are tracking the numbers of the clock face round with your eyes in a big wide circle. All the way round, which ever direction it doesn't matter. So tapping, thinking about those thoughts; I'm unsure I don't know where Mum is, I wish Mum was here and so on, and kinda really getting the sense of that in your body, and then slowly and comfortably moving the eyes in a big wide circle round. I'm not sure, I don't know where Mum is and so on. OK, stop the eyes and relax and move them in the other direction, and still seeing in that scene what was going on at that moment in time, feeling the feelings in your body. Just focus intensely on the feelings in your body, and the eyes slowly and comfortably round, OK. Good and relax the eyes and move them just one last time, slowly and comfortably in the other direction. Slowly and comfortably focusing intensely on that physical feeling, at that moment in time and breathe out for me, good, good. Relax the eyes, relax the hands. OK, good. So in your mind's eye run through from that point where you are coming down the stairs to the room and just tell me for that little chunk of the movie, coming down to the room if there's any kind of intensity in that little chunk, OK? Just take your time.

**G -** I don't know it doesn't seem . . . so important any more.

**Me -** Great. Anything going on in your physical body?

**G -** Relief.

**Me -** Relief. Is it like a zero?

**G -** Yeah.

**Me -** Yeah, cause if it's a half, I want to know that it's a half.

**G -** (Laughing) No, it's a zero.

**Me -** Good, so let's continue in the movie and as you, after you've gone into the room, tell me what's going on and what you are aware of emotionally the first time it kinda brings something up for you? Just take your time.

**G -** (pause). . . A can of beer beside his chair, and even though I was only six I was aware that he had a drinking problem.

**Me -** OK, as you are looking at that can of beer now what's the meaning there, there must be something there?

**G -** Fear.

**Me -** Fear, yeah, I was picking that up. (Client taps round points, repeating language, mirroring me) (UE) Under the eye. Does Dad's can of beer, does that kinda represent something? Does that kinda represent power or something else…I'm guessing here. But you know what I mean?

**G -** Umm, change.

**Me -** Change, OK. (UA) under the arm, (EB) eyebrow. So just freeze-frame on that can of beer OK and give me a number?

**G -** About 10.

**Me -** (TH) Top of the head. Breathe out, and put two fingertips on each eyebrow. Stay on the eyebrow point for me and keep tapping and I want you to go like this, I want you to go . . . (sudden and quick breath out) . . . I want you to breathe out really suddenly and really quickly as you see that can of beer and tap OK, just go (sudden and quick breath out).

**G -** (breath out)

**Me -** Good. OK, (SE) side of the eye, (UE) under the eye, good, good (CB). . . just see that can of beer . . . OK . . . OK . . . and with me, OK? (Client taps round points, repeating language, mirroring me) (KC) Even though I don't know what's going on in this situation…I am trying to understand, if I could make sense of this situation, that's all I want to do…but maybe, in this situation… I've forgotten about, all the situations, that led to this situation, all the situations that got me here to this point, and all the situations that got Dad here to this point…in this moment, I might only be considering, this moment, but as far as me and Dad are concerned, there are a lot of moments that led us to this moment, there is a lot of his stuff that has led us to this moment, and even though I'm not ready to, even though I don't want to forgive him, yet...there's a lot of his baggage that has brought him to this situation, it might just be possible, that his intentions, are loving, he might just be doing the best that he can, with what he's got. Because on a moment to moment basis… I know, that in the situations I'm dealt, I'm doing the best that I can, despite the fact that it might not look that way to others, and it might just be possible, that Dad is doing the best that he can, given the situation that he's got, and given all the situations he's been dealt with in the past, this is the only way he knows how to react, he's truly doing the best he can.

**Me -** OK, what's going on?  Have I totally traumatized you?

**G -** No. (Laughing).

**Me -** Is it possible though?  Is it?

**G -** Yeah.

**Me -** Maybe?

**G -** Yeah. (Laughing).

**Me -** 'Cause we've all got situations, you know, and . . . despite whatever it is… despite his behaviour in this situation, it's pretty foolhardy to say that we kinda get up in the morning and say *how can I really fuck today up?* or *how can I really fuck my daughter up today?* Or whatever, so, people do things that don't look, their behaviour is not very acceptable?  But their intentions, may be different, 'cause what you are doing in that moment in time, as we all are, is the best that you can, on the basis of, it's kinda like a bully, like a bully in the playground, they are trying to get love, trying to get attention, at home or whatever and they can't get it.  The only means, the only means, at that moment in time in the playground or whatever is by lashing out at others, because they have learned this is the way I get attention if I hit others, but the point is, in that moment in time, that is the point they've got to, to get that love.  See what I mean?

**G -** Uh-huh.

**Me -** OK.  So, have a breath out, have a relax and umm, have a look at the beer-can and just tell me what's going on for you.

**G -** Umm, just this feeling of disappointed, and worried because I don't . . . I don't really understand what . . . what the power of the drink does, I know that it changes him but could it kill him or...

**Me -** So it's kinda like . . . well there's a lot of stuff going on there so let's simplify it.  What's going on in your body, as you're aware of those emotions?  Do you feel a feeling in your body or can you find a feeling for me now? . . . OK, so let's just start with some general tapping, we won't bother saying anything just now, just focus on that physical feeling . . . good . . . I can kinda sense sadness, hurt is that . . .

**G -** Yeah.

**Me -** Yeah, OK.  I was going to say, I might put out a lot of stuff there and it might not hit the target and you can correct me; a couple of things to notice. First of all, you notice that you've maybe got a greater depth of recall of the event generally, you know what I mean?  Do you notice that you remember greater detail about the event now that you might not have thought of previously?

**G -** Yeah.

**Me -** And also we tend to . . . it is very typical that we shift aspects of, work through the anger and then we'll shift on to sadness or the hurt, you know what I mean?  Sometimes it can feel like we are tapping into these things and it's still there, but it's a different aspect and I just like to point that out so people notice that you know.  OK.  Good.  So relax and breathe out. What are you aware of now when you look at that same moment?

**G -** Umm . . . I don't know.  I still feel disappointed in him because I know that . . . I don't know, I know that he's human and . . . he makes mistakes just like everyone else, but I feel so let down . . . he was supposed to be looking after me and my brother and . . .  I don't even know if he's drunk or what.

**Me -** OK, (Client taps round points, repeating language, mirroring me) (TH) I feel let down, (EB) I feel let down, (SE) I'm disappointed in him... (UE) he's Dad... (UN) he should be doing better... (CH) I'm disappointed (CB) and sad... (UA) because I deserve better...

**Me -** Does it land with you now?

**G -** No.

**Me -** OK, (TH) this remaining sadness (EB) and disappointment (SE) I'm disappointed (UE) (UN) (CH) (CB) I'm disappointed (UA) just disappointed.

**Me -** Good. OK, give me a number for those kinda feelings; sadness disappointed and so on?

**G -** I'd say about 10.

**Me -** 10? OK, missed that one. OK, let's just keep tapping . . . where are you feeling it in your body?

**G -** In the chest.

**Me -** In the chest. OK (Client taps round points, repeating language, mirroring me). . . (EB) these chest feelings (CB) collar bone, these chest feelings. Does it feel . . . how does if feel? Tight? Loose? Big, Small?

**G -** Heavy.

**Me -** Heavy, OK. (CB) These heavy chest feelings.

**G -** These heavy chest feelings.

**Me -** Is it your heart?

**G -** Yeah.

**Me -** OK, (TH) this sadness (EB) this deep sadness… (SE) I want to understand, (UE) I want to understand, (UN) I'd like to understand, (CH) (CB) (UA) I'd like to understand, OK, let's do the finger points. It's next to the nail on each finger. OK, (TH) I'd like to understand…(IF) I don't yet… (MF) he's doing the best he can, (LF) maybe… (TH) even though it's a really shitty best, (IF) it's a really shitty best, (MF) I am six years old here, (LF) I'm doing the best I can to understand this… good breathe out. (EB) Two hands . . . remaining sadness, (SE) good, side of the eye, (UE) Good. Under the eye. Trying to understand, (UN) under the nose, trying to understand, (CH) remaining sadness, (CB) this sadness… (UA) this sadness. Breathe out . . . good, OK, give me a number, are we still a 10?

**G -** Umm, I'd say a 7.

**Me -** OK. Is there one kind of particular aspect about this that peaks that 7 or is there… . what sticks out for you?

**G -** Umm, I guess it's like . . . that moment is just . . . reminds me of every moment that he let me down.

**Me -** Right.

**G -** Every time he wasn't there and should have been.

**Me -** OK. (Client taps round points, repeating language, mirroring me) (KC) Even though this moment, reminds me of all those moments, and I don't particularly want to remember those moments...I accept me anyway, despite this situation. I'm OK... I survived, these feelings in my body are just energy, like anything else...I survived. Do you think it's like umm . . . in this scene, what are you focusing on? As you talk about, as you were talking there, him sitting there reminds me of . . . what are you seeing? Are you seeing him slumped in a chair.

**G -** Yes.

**Me -** OK. So . . . give me a number? Are we still at a 7 or 8?

**G -** Yeah.

**Me** - OK, let's do some tapping. OK, (Client taps round points, repeating language, mirroring me) (TH) Seeing him slumped in the chair, (EB) he's there slumped in the chair, (SE) he's there slumped in the chair... (UE) he's there slumped in the chair, (UN) good, and I'm trying to make sense of it, (CH) he's slumped in the chair, (CB) and I'm judging him, (UA) because that's what we do, (WR) because that's what I do, I judge him, (TH) and he judges me... (EB) I judge him based on my experiences... (SE) and my expectations, (UE) and he judges me based on his...(UN) 'cause that's all we've got to go on, (CH) he's slumped on the chair... (CB) remaining sadness, (UA) remaining sadness... (WR) remaining sadness. Good, breathe out. Give me a number for the sadness?

**G** - 4.

**Me** - 4, and is it still in the heart or has it moved... has it changed .. ?

**G** - No.

**Me** - Where ever it is, where ever it is, close the eyes and I want you to hold the intention, and hold the want, internally, as a state... (pause) enter a place, internally, that the feeling is just going to soften. This physical feeling. Allow the physical feeling to soften and flow, it's just energy, (pause) it's just energy . . . just allow the feeling to soften and as it softens it will flow (pause), and I want you to imagine the top of your head opens up and a solvent liquid of some kind like water or sunshine or rose quartz water just flows all the way down through your head and goes all the way to the source of this feeling and just works it's way and pulsates it and massages it and disperses it and softens and just allows the feeling to soften and flow (pause) . . . soften and flow . . . soften and flow (pause) . . . even softer, softer still (pause), softer still allow it to flow, soften and flow (pause) . . . even softer . . . even softer . . . softer still . . . softer still (pause). . . OK, and with your attention and focus on the physical feeling tell me what's happening.

**G -** . . . it's gone.

**Me -** Is it like a zero or . . .

**G -** Yeah.

**Me -** So in your mind's eye take a look at him slumped in the chair and just tell me what's going on in your body emotionally?

**G -** . . . I just feel sad.

**Me -** Sad.

**G -** I don't feel like I'm tense.

**Me -** Just feel it in your body and hold the want, hold the intention and focus, soften the feeling (pause). . . softer still . . . softer still . . . softer still . . . see him sitting in that chair, soften the feeling (pause). . . OK, soften and flow . . . softer still . . . OK, softer still . . . soften and flow. . . look at him now in the chair, just focus on the physical feeling and tell me what's happening?

**G -** Nothing.

**Me -** OK. So continue the movie after that point and just tell me when something comes up for you?

**G -** . . . umm . . . sitting at the side of the chair . . . there was a film on and I can't remember what exactly was going on in the film but I just remember being really, really frightened by it.

**Me -** OK, (Client taps round points, repeating language, mirroring me) so start tapping, top of the head. (TH) Really frightened... (EB) really frightened. (SE) Give me a number... like 20?

**G -** (Laughing) Nearer 8.

**Me -** (UE) Nearer 8, under the eye, really frightened. Is it in the tummy or is it?

**G -** Yeah.

**Me -** OK, just shift slightly, directly under the pupil. That's it. OK, this fear.

**G -** This fear.

**Me -** Feel it in your physical body. This fear, (UE) under the eye . . . (CB) collar bone . . . breathe out . . . give me a number for the feeling?

**G -** 4.

**Me -** 4, OK. With that 4, what are you aware of, what are you focusing on?

**G -** . . . sitting by the side of the chair, feeling alone.

**Me -** Feeling alone, OK. (Client taps round points, repeating language, mirroring me) (TH) Feeling alone, (EB) feeling alone (SE) sitting by the side of the chair... (UE) feeling alone, (UN) are you holding on to the chair, or are you sitting down beside it? (client nods) Sitting down beside it . . . (CH) by the side of the chair (CB) feeling alone, (UA) feeling all these feelings, (WR) by the side of the chair. OK . . . anything going on anywhere? Physical body?

**G -** No.

**Me -** So just kinda of really put yourself into that moment, being aware of sitting by the side of the chair, maybe aware of the colour of the floor covering and the dimensions of the room and tell me what comes up.

**G -** It's just really dark, just the light off the TV.

**Me -** The light from the TV.

**G -** The chair that I'm sitting beside is really, really high and I look really, really small next to it and I can't see any of my Dad next to me in the chair.

**Me -** (TH) This high chair... (EB) it's really dark, (SE) I'm beside this high chair (UE) and it's dark... (UN) I can't see Dad... (CH) behind this high chair, (CB) I'm aware of the TV, (UA) and it's dark...So let's do this one again where we move the eyes, OK, and just set yourself in that situation and just be aware of the TV and aware of the darkness, be aware of the side of the chair, be aware of the floor covering and spin the eyes round slowly and comfortably... (pause) and relax the eyes and move them in the other direction and repeat with me. (tapping gamut) I'm sitting here, in this dark, I'm aware of the height of the chair, and the film, I can't see Dad. Good. Relax the eyes and spin them in the other direction. I'm aware of the height of the chair...I can't see Dad. . . breathe out. Relax the eyes, relax the hands. Have a drink of water there. . . . umm . . . Just consider that moment again for me, and just tell me if it has changed or if anything is happening for you?

**G -** . . . feel safer.

**Me -** Feel safer. Has the darkness changed at all?

**G -** Yeah strangely, it's more of a, I don't know, more of a blue light.

**Me -** You feel slightly safer. Give me a number from 0 to 10 for whatever is left?

**G -** About half.

**Me -** Half, OK . . . umm . . . what would you say that half is?

**G -** Probably still a bit of fear.

**Me -** Fear, OK. (Client taps round points, repeating language, mirroring me) (TH) remaining fear... (EB) sitting in this place... (SE) next to Dad, (UE) remaining fear... (UN) breathe out, (CH) remaining fear, (TH) the fingers. Remaining fear. (IF) This half in my . . . where do you feel it?

**G -** In my chest.

**Me -** (MF) (LF) This half in my chest, (TH) this half feeling in my chest, (EB) this remaining fear... (SE) this remaining fear, (UE) as I sit here, (UN) in this room, (CH) I'm aware of the chair... (CB) (UA) ...aware of the chair, breathe out . . . OK, still a half?

**G -** No.

**Me -** A zero?

**G -** Yes.

**Me -** Certain?

**G -** Yes.

**Me -** OK, so, umm let's run through the next moment that bothers you.

**G -** To be honest that's all it was, that's the . . .

**Me -** All the movie?

**G -** Yeah.

**Me -** OK, so, I'm very thorough. Go back to the start of the movie for me and just run through in your mind's eye at a nice leisurely pace take your time going through it and look for anything that is there because it gives us an opportunity to clear, just look for anything at all, even if it's just a quarter, OK?

**G -** (pause) No, everything is OK.

**Me -** OK. Does that, does it, what are you aware of physically? Is there…

**G -** Release.

**Me -** Great, OK. Well, I think we could leave it there for today as we've made some progress on that movie and it seems like a natural place to draw a line under things… generally speaking, what we're doing here, is picking away at the experiences underneath the anxiety you know. That's how we pull it out at the root cause. And if we take out one or two biggies it can begin a kind of emotional domino effect in our favour, you know? Do you get that sense?

**G -** Yeah definitely.

**Me -** I'm not saying we're performing miracles here but usually once we have taken away, you know, half a dozen memories, something like that, you can actually get to see the bigger picture; and thinking, cognition begins to change on a daily basis you know what I mean.

**G -** Yeah.

**Me -** So you've got all the EFT points, you know, so you could do it now yourself, it's just, if you get into some heavy stuff, it's nice to have someone around to guide you.

**G -** Yeah.

**Me -** But, by all means try it out, maybe don't pick out a 20, pick out a 6 of a memory and see how you get on, and come back and see me if need be.

**G -** It was really enjoyable. OK. Thank you.

**Me -** Thanks for coming in today.

# Appendix : Running Start Guide

## *Running Start Guide:*

I present here a shortcut version of EFT, which is the main one I use in a clinic setting. Very rarely do I add in the 9 gamut procedure of the full basic recipe, but for completeness, or if you need to, it's freely available at http://www.emofree.com/downloadeftmanual.htm as part of Gary Craig's get started manual.

## *Basic EFT Procedure*

1) Choose a problem to work on, e.g. anxiety about a visit to the dentist.

2) Tune in to the problem, and rate your emotional or physical discomfort using the SUDS(subjective units of distress scale) scale of 0-10, where 0=no distress and 10=highest level of discomfort.

3) State the setup statement below out loud, 3 times, whilst continuously tapping the KC point, or rubbing the sore spot. (Figure 2)

> *Even though I (have this dentist anxiety), I deeply and profoundly love and accept myself.*

4) Tap about 7 times on each of the following points whilst repeating a suitable reminder phrase at each point, e.g. *this dentist anxiety* (Figure 1)

TH, EB, SE, UE, UN, CH, CB, UA

5) Then, tap on the finger points, below, still repeating the same reminder phrase at each point. (Figure 2)

TH, IF, MF, LF

6) Rate SUDS level again.

7) Repeat 2-5 until full relief achieved.


Optionally, I also use the wrist point (WR), on the inside of the wrist around the pulse area, as one of my favourite points.

Generally, for best results, be specific, be persistent, and apply EFT to *all* aspects of a problem for full relief.

For info, tapping on the top of the head, then the inside wrist, then the inner ankle will cover all 14 meridians with just three points.

## *Figure 1 – Body Points*

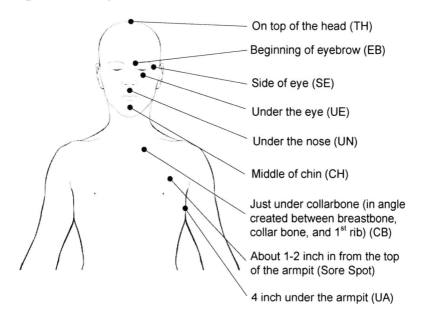

On top of the head (TH)

Beginning of eyebrow (EB)

Side of eye (SE)

Under the eye (UE)

Under the nose (UN)

Middle of chin (CH)

Just under collarbone (in angle created between breastbone, collar bone, and 1$^{st}$ rib) (CB)

About 1-2 inch in from the top of the armpit (Sore Spot)

4 inch under the armpit (UA)

## *Figure 2 – Hand Points*

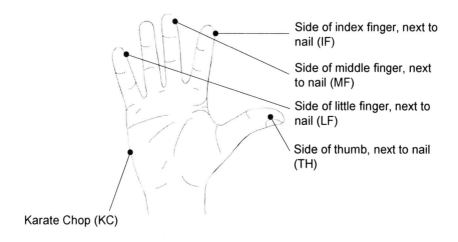

Side of index finger, next to nail (IF)

Side of middle finger, next to nail (MF)

Side of little finger, next to nail (LF)

Side of thumb, next to nail (TH)

Karate Chop (KC)

Notes

## Chapter 3

1 – "How to apply EFT when there are no clear, specific memories to tap on" by Stefan Gonick. http://www.emofree.com/Articles2/trauma-T-t.htm

## Chapter 4

1 – "Self sabotage - healing the parts that don't want to heal" by Jaqui Crooks. http://www.emofree.com/Articles2/self-sabotage-parts.htm

## Chapter 6

1 – "Time and Reframing: An Easy Technique that Generates Fast Results" by Tania Prince. http://www.emofree.com/Articles2/time-reframing-tania.htm. Reproduced with permission.

## Chapter 7

1 – Excerpts from Chapter 17 - "How to Get What You Want And Want What You Have" by John Gray. ISBN – 0091826500. Reproduced with permission.

2 – "The "Turbo-Tapping" Technique" by Ryan N. Harrison, MA, HHP, NC, EFT-ADV. http://www.emofree.com/articles/turbo-tapping.htm

## Chapter 10

1 – "Dr. Patricia Carrington's use of "Choices" in the EFT Setup Phrase" - by Dr. Patricia Carrington. http://www.emofree.com/articles/choices.htm

Resources

## Free Websites

| | |
|---|---|
| http://www.emofree.com | Resource-rich and highly acclaimed website of the EFT Founder Gary Craig. A must-see. |
| http://www.emofree.com/downloadeftmanual.htm | Download your free EFT manual from the EFT website |
| http://www.stressreliefclinic.co.uk | My site |
| http://www.masteringeft.com | Home of EFT Master Patricia Carrington and the EFT 1-Minute Newsletter |

## Find An EFT Practitioner

| | |
|---|---|
| http://www.emofree.com/Practitioners/referralMain.asp | Per Gary Craig's site |
| http://www.uoom.com/aamet/practitioner.php | AAMET site |
| http://www.masteringeft.com/EFTPR/PractitionerList.htm | Patricia Carrington's site |

## EFT Discussion Groups

| | |
|---|---|
| http://health.groups.yahoo.com/group/Meridian-Energy/ | AAMET discussion group |

| http://health.groups.yahoo.com/group/meridiantherapy/ | AMT discussion group |
| http://eftcommunity.emofree.com/forums/ | Gary Craig's Emofree Forums |

## EFT Training

| http://www.efttrainingcourses.net | Home of Karl Dawson's EFT UK training. Highly recommended. |
| http://www.eft-courses.co.uk/ | Tania Prince, EFT Master & Trainer |
| http://www.emotional-freedom-technique.net/ | Home of Jaqui Crooks, EFT Master & Trainer |

## Books

| Sleight of Mouth – Robert Dilts | ISBN 0916990478 |
| Mind-lines: Lines For Changing Minds - L. Michael Hall Bobby G. Bodenhamer | ISBN 1890001155 |
| Frame Games: Persuasion Excellence - L. Michael Hall | ISBN 1890001198 |